BISON
BOOKS

Other titles by Robert M. Utley
available in Bison Books editions

BILLY THE KID: A SHORT AND VIOLENT LIFE

FRONTIER REGULARS: THE UNITED STATES ARMY AND THE INDIAN

FRONTIERSMEN IN BLUE: THE UNITED STATES ARMY AND THE INDIAN,
1848–1865

LIFE IN CUSTER'S CAVALRY: DIARIES AND LETTERS OF ALBERT AND
JENNIE BARNITZ, 1867–1868 (ED. UTLEY)

CUSTER

AND THE
GREAT CONTROVERSY

THE ORIGIN AND DEVELOPMENT OF A LEGEND

ROBERT M. UTLEY

Introduction to the Bison Books Edition
by Brian W. Dippie

UNIVERSITY OF NEBRASKA PRESS

LINCOLN AND LONDON

⊗ The paper in this book meets the minimum requirements of
American National Standard for Information Sciences—Permanence
of Paper for Printed Library materials, ANSI Z39.48-1984.

First Bison Books printing: 1998
Most recent printing indicated by the last digit below:
10   9   8   7   6   5   4   3   2   1

Library of Congress Cataloging-in-Publication Data
Utley, Robert Marshall, 1929–
Custer and the great controversy: the origin and development of a
legend / by Robert M. Utley; introduction to the Bison Books edition
by Brian W. Dippie.
p. cm.
Originally published: Los Angeles: Westernlore Press, 1962.
Includes bibliographical references (p.) and index.
ISBN 0-8032-9561-8 (pbk.: alkaline paper)
1. Custer, George Armstrong, 1830–1876. 2. Little Bighorn, Battle of
the, Mont., 1876. I. Title.
E83.876.U79   1998
973.8'2—dc21
97-48398   CIP

Reprinted from the original 1962 edition by Westernlore Press,
Pasadena, California.

To the Luces . . .
For many cherished memories of Custer Hill

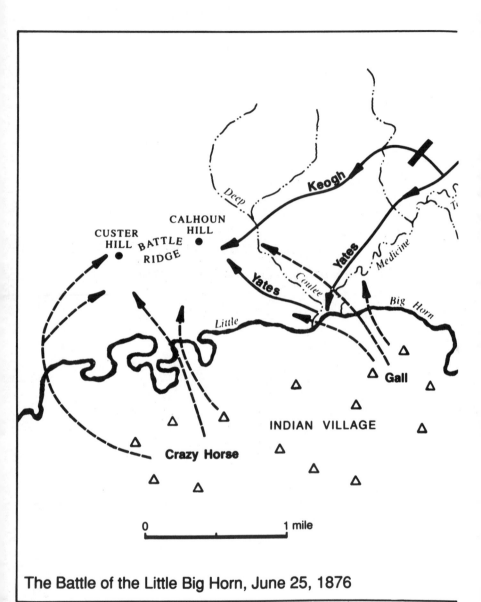

The Battle of the Little Big Horn, June 25, 1876

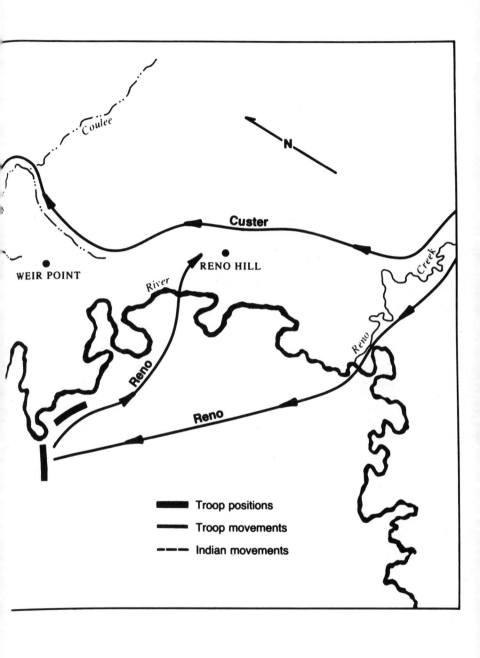

Coulee

N

Custer

WEIR POINT

RENO HILL

River

Creek

Reno

Reno

Reno

Troop positions

Troop movements

--- Indian movements

INTRODUCTION

Brian W. Dippie

In the emotional aftermath of George Armstrong Custer's crushing defeat on the Little Bighorn River in Montana Territory on June 25, 1876, newspapers published a poetic outpouring by the celebrated (Walt Whitman) and the obscure. The *New York Herald* was no exception. On July 15, it carried (anonymously) a 147-line contribution by one of its staff members, Joseph I. C. Clarke, titled "Custer's Last Charge." Clarke had met Custer shortly before he headed west to lead the Seventh Cavalry in the field and was aware of the political controversy that dogged him after his falling out with President Ulysses Grant over scandals in the War Department. Consequently, Clarke's poem portrayed Custer riding to the Little Bighorn resolved that

> "Death is better than shame or doubt—
>   Better because of the name I bore.
> Right seems Wrong when the right's disgraced,
>   When the honor I bear in my heart's mid-core
> Is touched by a jeer, when my name displaced
>   Is a jibe for the varlets at Caesar's door.
> Life worth living means shame effaced—
>   Means Custer higher than e'er before;
> And there, by my mother's God I swear,
>   Lies a bloody balm for my trampled pride.
> What a devil would dream of will Custer dare!"
>   And he pointed over the high divide.

Affecting that tone of infinite condescension calculated to annoy Americans, an English journalist critiqued Clarke's poem:

Being very angry at politicians in Washington, Custer revenged himself by rushing headlong into an ambush. This is what the poem comes
to in plain English. . . . His "voice like a clear trumpet sound" is heard
and answered by a cheer; but shouting, it may be feared, never gained
a battle, although sometimes it may have helped to lose one. Indeed,
if General Custer had nothing better to say than the poet says for him,
we might think that on that memorable morning he was, as our police
reports say, "considerably under the influence of liquor." Ultimately,
however, he left off talking, which seems to have been the only sen-
sible thing he did, and "his last cry was his rifle's deep tone." Amid
"heroes' gore," "corpses," "spouting wounds," and "savage foes," he
made a perfectly melodramatic end. If we believe this writer, General
Custer was promoted not only to the full extent of his dessert, but far
beyond it. The leader of a "wild, mad dash" at an ambushed enemy ought
never to have been allowed to lead at all. But perhaps General Custer was
not such a fool as he looks in poetry.[1]

Perhaps—perhaps not. In that proposition is the essence of the
Custer controversy and of a popular fascination with Custer's Last
Stand that, after 121 years, shows no sign of abating.

Thirty-five years ago Robert M. Utley published *Custer and the
Great Controversy*. What strikes me most on rereading the book is
the clarity of Utley's prose and the precision with which he cuts
through the dense tangle of Custeriana. Studies of popular legends and myths, based as they are on contradictory and repetitive
material, can themselves be convoluted and repetitious; tedious
summary often overwhelms analysis. Here, Utley succinctly traces
the growing Custer controversy from its earliest sources: newspaper accounts, the military and political fallout over responsibility,
and the biography by Frederick Whittaker rushed into print a few
months after Custer's death (our age did not invent the instant
biography).

More remarkable is the fact that *Custer and the Great Controversy*
is the work of a very young historian. Essentially, it is Utley's master's
thesis, "The Custer Controversy: An Historiographical Study of the
Battle of the Little Big Horn for the Period 1876–1900," completed
at the University of Indiana in 1952, when he was twenty-two. As a
seventh grader, Utley had been smitten by the most famous movie

Custer of them all, Errol Flynn's romantic cavalier hero in *They Died with Their Boots On* (1941). He just had to learn the truth behind that shining screen image. Thus a historian was born, and "The Custer Controversy" eventually followed. Utley published a chapter from it in *North Dakota History* in 1955, "The Custer Battle in the Contemporary Press," and outlined his thesis proper in "The Legend of the Little Bighorn," published in the journal of the Potomac Corral of the Westerners the next year. That might have been it for the Custer controversy, since Utley, having completed his military service as historian with the Joint Chiefs of Staff, had begun in 1957 his distinguished twenty-three-year career with the National Park Service and was immersed in writing a history of the Battle of Wounded Knee that would appear in 1963 as *The Last Days of the Sioux Nation.*[2]

Fortunately for students of the Custer battle, a friend from California, Hugh W. Shick, "pestered" Utley into submitting his master's thesis for publication. The present book is the happy result. Today, Utley regards it, fondly, as one might a youthful indiscretion, but for once I get to say Bob Utley is wrong. Readers of this new edition of *Custer and the Great Controversy* will find themselves agreeing with Hugh Shick that his "goading was justified; . . . [Utley's] efforts come forth honest and unbiased."[3]

Utley has since changed or qualified his position on some issues in light of subsequent findings. For example, he has retracted his objections to the Mary Adams affidavit. "Until recently most students thought this affidavit spurious because they did not believe that Mary Adams accompanied the expedition," he commented in 1988. "Now she is known to have been with Custer."[4] His position on the most celebrated of all sole survivors, the Crow scout Curley, has advanced beyond the cautious observation made here that Curley's story is "not without a certain indirect merit" to a positive endorsement in 1991 of the research of John S. Gray. He now thinks that "Gray penetrates the fog, makes sense of Curley's testimony, shows him to have been at Custer's side all the way to Calhoun Hill, where the final half-hour of the Last Stand began, and validates his claim to have watched the end from a distance."[5]

Utley would still counsel caution in relying on the Indian accounts of the battle. But his own 1993 biography of Sitting Bull, *The Lance and the Shield*, demonstrates how a discriminating and judicious use of Indian sources can produce a superior history, and a number of recent books on the battle have fulfilled his prediction that Indian testimony, properly used, will help "unravel the enigma of the Little Bighorn."[6]

Corrections and updates do not alter a simple fact: *Custer and the Great Controversy* is a seminal work. It still provides the best concise introduction to the issues central to the dauntingly vast body of Custer literature. Start here, and everything else falls into place. By tracing the "branches from the Whittaker tree," Utley sets up the twentieth-century historical debate pitting Custerphiles and Custerphobes. Much ink devoted to the Little Bighorn has flowed since 1962, and new facts and new speculations abound. But the old polarities persist. However dense its foliage today, the Custer controversy remains a recognizable outgrowth from those nineteenth-century seeds. Since Utley, many historians have scrutinized aspects of the Custer legend. Now book-length studies examine the role of Elizabeth Custer in polishing her husband's halo, the legend of the horse Comanche and the Irish-born captain who rode him, and the enormous body of art, fiction, poetry, and film that constitutes the "Custer myth."[7] All can be fairly characterized as branches from the Utley tree.

Robert M. Utley has a direct, businesslike approach to writing history that transforms laborious research into effortless reading. He is the consummate professional. Consequently I am passing along two excellent pieces of advice he has given me that I have managed to ignore, but from which others might be wise enough to profit. First, Utley says, always meet your deadlines. Missing deadlines makes life so miserable that the only logical option is to not miss them. Second, do not brood about writing—*write*. A tendency to brood ensures missing deadlines, which ensures more brooding. Get on with it, Bob Utley says, and the result of that no-nonsense philosophy is a body of work as impressive in its scope and volume as in its excellence.

Although Utley has gone on to publish outstanding books about Billy the Kid and Sitting Bull and, most recently, a history of the mountain men, he remains best known for his leadership in the field of frontier military history. His first love, the Custer legend, continues to be a compelling interest. In 1976, amid swirling controversy, he stepped into the breach to deliver the major address during the ceremonies at the Custer Battlefield National Monument commemorating the centennial of the Battle of the Little Bighorn. In an atmosphere heavy with the potential for confrontation, even violence, Utley made his point:

> The fact is that history, like life, is complex, contradictory, and ambiguous. There are few genuine heroes or villains in real life, merely people who are sometimes heroic, sometimes villainous, but most of the time simply human. Such were the soldiers and the Indians who fought here on June 25, 1876. . . .
>
> . . . we should dedicate ourselves in this bicentennial and centennial year to righting the wrongs of the past. But in reaching for that goal, let us not infuse this battlefield with a modern meaning untrue to the past. Let us not bend it artificially to serve contemporary needs and ends, however laudable. Let us accept it and understand it on its own terms, not ours. As we shall want posterity to look back at us, so we ourselves must look back at those who have preceded us.[8]

In 1986 Utley went on record with his reservations about the archaeological digs at the battlefield (unjustified, he argued, and in contravention of park policy), and in 1992 he took a supportive position on the name change that saw the Custer Battlefield become the Little Bighorn Battlefield National Monument, recognizing that it was simply the latest in the succession of controversies that have always shaped the Custer legend:

> For the past twenty years, and for the indefinite future, this place where historic site and shrine come together has been, is, and will continue to be a battleground for a struggle between two patriotisms. I do not see the battle being won by either side in my lifetime. But I live with it more comfortably now, for I console myself that I am a historian watching the unfolding of history.[9]

There is no final word, no end to the Custer debate, then. But there is a beginning point, and readers of *Custer and the Great Controversy* hold the key in their hands.

NOTES

1. "General Custer," *Saturday Review* 42 (July 29, 1876): 135.
2. See Robert M. Utley, "But for Custer's Sins," *Western Historical Quarterly* 2 (October 1971): 357–62; John M. Carroll and Mike Harrison, eds., *The Robert M. Utley Bibliographic Checklist* (Mattituck NY: J. M. Carroll Company, 1983); "Western History Association Prize Recipient, 1988: Robert M. Utley," *Western Historical Quarterly* 20 (May 1989): 133–39; Sierra Adare, "Robert Utley Offers a Wild and Perilous Journey with the West's Most Famous Mountain Men," *Wild West* 10 (October 1997): 80, 82, 84.
3. Hugh W. Shick to Brian W. Dippie, [September 9, 1967].
4. Robert M. Utley, *Cavalier in Buckskin: George Armstrong Custer and the Western Military Frontier* (Norman: University of Oklahoma Press, 1988), 195.
5. Robert M. Utley, foreword to John S. Gray, *Custer's Last Campaign: Mitch Boyer and the Little Bighorn Reconstructed* (Lincoln: University of Nebraska Press, 1991), x–xi.
6. Richard G. Hardorff, *Hokahey! A Good Day to Die: The Indian Casualties of the Custer Fight* (Spokane WA: Arthur H. Clark, 1993), and his two compilations *Lakota Recollections of the Custer Fight: New Sources of Indian-Military History* (Spokane WA: Arthur H. Clark, 1991) and *Cheyenne Memories of the Custer Fight: A Source Book* (Spokane WA: Arthur H. Clark, 1995) (both now available as Bison Books); Jerome A. Greene, comp., *Lakota and Cheyenne: Indian Views of the Great Sioux War, 1876–1877* (Norman: University of Oklahoma Press, 1994); and Gregory F. Michno, *Lakota Noon: The Indian Narrative of Custer's Defeat* (Missoula MT: Mountain Press Publishing Company, 1997). Richard Allan Fox Jr.'s revisionist *Archaeology, History, and Custer's Last Battle: The Little Bighorn Reexamined* (Norman: University of Oklahoma Press, 1993) also relies heavily on Indian testimony.
7. See, for example, Shirley A. Leckie, *Elizabeth Bacon Custer and the Making of a Myth* (Norman: University of Oklahoma Press, 1993); Elizabeth Atwood Lawrence, *His Very Silence Speaks: Comanche—The Horse Who Survived Custer's Last Stand* (Detroit: Wayne State University Press, 1989);

and Brian W. Dippie, *Custer's Last Stand: The Anatomy of an American Myth* (1976; reprint, Lincoln: University of Nebraska Press, 1994). The myth now occupies a place of its own in modern Custer scholarship: see Paul Andrew Hutton, ed., *The Custer Reader* (Lincoln: University of Nebraska Press, 1992), and Charles E. Rankin, ed., *Legacy: New Perspectives on the Battle of the Little Bighorn* (Helena: Montana Historical Society Press, 1996).

8. Remarks by Robert M. Utley, News Release, U.S. Department of the Interior, National Park Service, Rocky Mountain Regional Office, Denver CO, June 24, 1976.

9. Robert M. Utley, "On Digging Up Custer Battlefield," *Montana: The Magazine of Western History* 36 (spring 1986): 80–82; and Utley, "Whose Shrine Is It?: The Ideological Struggle for Custer Battlefield," *Montana: The Magazine of Western History* 42 (winter 1992): 70–74.

Table of Contents

Illustrations

Foreword

THE BIBLIOGRAPHY OF THE Battle of the Little Bighorn has grown to voluminous proportions, and continues to grow year by year. Each addition is ordinarily heralded as "the Custer book to end Custer books," or "the last word on the subject." In one sense, then, this is not another Custer book, for I do not aspire to offer the last word on the subject. Rather, this book is a history of many last words on the subject. For students of the Little Bighorn, I hope that it will not only trace the origins and development of the Custer Controversy, but will also suggest why there will never be a last word.

Santa Fe, New Mexico,
December 1961.

Acknowledgments

MANY PEOPLE CONTRIBUTED in many ways to the completion of this work. Among those whom I would thank especially are Dr. O. O. Winther, Professor of History at Indiana University; Dr. Kathryn M. Troxell, custodian of the Robert S. Ellison collection of Western Americana at Indiana University Library; Maj. Edward S. Luce, former superintendent of Custer Battlefield National Monument, and Mrs. Luce; the late Col. W. A. Graham of Pacific Palisades, Calif.; Dr. Lawrence A. Frost, Monroe, Mich.; the late Fred Dustin, Saginaw, Mich.; the late Dr. Charles Kuhlman, Billings, Mont.; R. G. Cartwright, Lead, S. Dak.; Roy P. Johnson, Fargo, N. Dak.; Roy E. Appleman, Washington, D. C.; James S. Hutchins, University of Arizona; and Dr. Norman Maclean, Professor of English, University of Chicago.

To Walter T. Vitous of Olympia, Wash., who prepared the maps; and to Hugh Shick of Hollywood, Calif., who pestered me into submitting this for publication, my particular thanks are due.

Chapter I

THE BACKGROUND

ON JUNE 25, 1876, LT. COL. George A. Custer, Brevet Major General, U. S. Army, and five troops of the Seventh U. S. Cavalry perished at the hands of Sioux and Cheyenne warriors on the banks of the Little Bighorn River, in southern Montana. The other seven troops of the regiment, Maj. Marcus A. Reno commanding, survived a two-day siege atop bluffs lining the east bank of the river four miles to the south. Judged by standards of warfare in the nuclear age, the Battle of the Little Bighorn was an insignificant border skirmish, for only 263 men were slain. Yet published material dealing with the engagement instantly began rolling off the nation's presses, and has continued in an undiminished stream today reaching truly extraordinary proportions.

Custer and the Great Controversy

Few events in American history have caught the public fancy so forcibly as the Custer disaster; few have inspired such intensity of interest and argument; and few have been more clouded by the producers of legend and fiction. The result is a historical debate beside which all others pale. No national or professional boundaries limit the cult of Little Bighorn enthusiasts—men and women who love nothing more than to immerse themselves in the historical records of this Indian fight on the remote Montana frontier of 1876, and to argue over evidence that will never conclusively answer the mystifying questions that make up the Custer Controversy: Did Custer disobey Terry's orders? Did Reno abandon Custer to his fate? What happened on the Custer Battlefield? What manner of man was George Armstrong Custer? These are the central questions of the Custer Controversy.

The Custer Controversy sprang from a complex of historical circumstances, not least of which was the death, in that last bloody struggle on Custer Hill, of the key witnesses who might have shed crucial illumination upon the questions historians would ask. But there were other circumstances, too. A muddled press coverage of the Sioux War of 1876, followed by a bitter editorial campaign, waged chiefly for partisan political reasons, laid the foundation of controversy and error. Popular writers wrote from press accounts and thus circulated much misinformation. In large measure this led to a demand for fixing blame on someone for such an unprecedented disaster. Then came the Reno Court of Inquiry and the "great debate" that participants in the Sioux War carried on for the rest of their lives. The literature of the Little Bighorn mushroomed. In the public mind, fabrications invented by ingenious dime novelists became historical truth. Recriminations grew more bitter. The truth became increasingly difficult to expose. When the Sioux finally collapsed under military pressure, they added yet another element of confusion, Indian testimony. All these factors shaped the unfolding history of the Little Bighorn.

The origin and growth of the Custer Controversy can best be understood by exploring four different aspects of the story: the press, the military "great debate," the Indian contributions, and the blossoming of legend and myth. We shall not have answered the central questions, but we shall, perhaps, have come to understand why they are unanswerable.

✗   ✗   ✗

The controversy cannot be understood unless one understands something of the dominant personalities of the Seventh Cavalry, the foremost of which resided in George Armstrong Custer.

He was born in New Rumley, Ohio, on December 5, 1839. Although a native of Ohio and appointed to the U. S. Military Academy by an Ohio congressman, he adopted Michigan as his home, and passed his early years on the shores of Lake Erie at Monroe. Dropped from West Point into the midst of the Civil War in 1861, Custer spent two years first as a cavalry lieutenant and then as aide to Gen. George B. McClellan before rising suddenly to fame and position. He made his debut at Gettysburg—a dashing 23-year-old officer with flowing yellow hair and the stars of a brigadier general sewed to the shoulders of his gold-encrusted, black velveteen uniform. From that day in 1863, when he led his Michigan cavalry brigade in a headlong charge on Wade Hampton's Confederate cavalry, to the June Sunday in 1876 when two Sioux bullets ended his brief but spectacular career, Custer was one of the most controversial and enigmatic personalities of his time. Emerging from the war with a brilliant record and the rank of major general, he was mustered out of the volunteers and assigned the Lieutenant Colonelcy of the newly organized regular Seventh Cavalry regiment.

On the plains his exploits compelled only slightly less public attention, and he eagerly set out to build a reputation in Indian fighting that would exceed his war record. Court-martialed and suspended for a year in 1867, he returned in 1868 to score a triumph by a brilliant attack on Black Kettle's Cheyenne village on the Washita in November. Whether campaigning against Kiowas and Comanches in Kansas or against the Sioux on the Yellowstone, the Boy General turned Indian fighter succeeded in keeping his name before the nation. His deeds of valor, his feats of sportsmanship, and his literary pursuits were extolled by an admiring press and followed with avidity by a hero-worshipping public.

But he also made enemies, many of whom did not harbor their enmity in private. He had a unique quality that inspired either love or hate, but never indifference.

The Background

There was no middle ground in anything that concerned George Armstrong Custer. When he led five troops of the Seventh Cavalry down the Little Bighorn to glory and immortality, his associates had already formed those conflicting views of his personality that were to make for bitter contention later.

Of radically different stamp was Marcus Albert Reno, born of a distinguished family in Carrolton, Illinois, in the spring of 1835. Graduating from West Point in 1857, five years before Custer, he was commissioned Colonel of the 12th Pennsylvania Cavalry in 1861. The close of the war found him in the same grade, but with an impressive record and a brevet of brigadier general. In 1868 he received an appointment as one of three majors in the Seventh Cavalry. When the regiment descended the Little Bighorn watershed on June 25, 1876, Reno was the only major on duty and second in command. He was also on the eve of his first Indian fight. Quiet and unassuming, far from gregarious, he had made little impression upon the regiment, either favorable or unfavorable. The Battle of the Little Bighorn would ruin his career and ultimately his self-respect.

In a regiment with a full complement of striking temperaments, Capt. Frederick William Benteen ranked second only to his commanding officer. Shrewd, cold and calculating, embittered toward humanity, he was steel-nerved under fire. He became an example of military proficiency after which many young subalterns, later to wear stars on their shoulders, patterned themselves. Benteen rose to Lieutenant Colonel of the Tenth

Missouri Cavalry during the war and was mustered out of the service the Colonel of a colored infantry regiment in 1866. The same year he was appointed a captain in the Seventh Cavalry. Perhaps inevitably, the Custer and Benteen personalities met head on. An open rupture came in 1869, and Benteen never, to the end of his life, relaxed his bitter animosity toward Custer.

Such were the principal military actors in the drama of the Little Bighorn. While they were yet campaigning in Kansas and Indian Territory, events were taking shape in the Northwest that would culminate in the tragedy in which they became controversial participants.

X   X   X

In 1868, a few months before the Seventh embarked upon the Washita adventure on the southern plains, the principal bands of Sioux and Cheyennes of the northern plains gathered at Fort Laramie to conclude with the United States the Treaty of 1868. This pact brought to a close, on terms highly favorable to the Sioux, the bloody Red Cloud War. The Laramie Treaty provided for creation of the Great Sioux Reservation, embracing that part of the present state of South Dakota west of the Missouri River. Here those Indians who desired could settle near fixed agencies under the administration of the Bureau of Indian Affiairs. The treaty also, however, set aside as unceded Indian territory a vast tract of land vaguely limited to "that country north of the North Platte River and east of the summits of the Big Horn Mountains." Many of the Sioux elected to settle near the agencies and receive the largess of the Indian Bureau. Others, under the nominal leadership of the Hunkpapa medicine man Sitting Bull, remained in the unceded territory, stonily rejecting all overtures from the Government. This arrangement would have been agreeable to all but for the westward march of the white man.

In 1872 and 1873 engineering parties, guarded by strong military escorts, penetrated the Yellowstone Valley of Montana to survey a route for the Northern Pacific Railroad, which had reached Bismarck and the Missouri River. The wild Sioux of the region understood from past experience the implications of a railroad. They contested the advance of the surveyors and exacted a slight toll in casualties. The next summer, 1874, an exploring expedition under Custer invaded the Black Hills of southwestern Dakota Territory, on the Great Sioux Reservation. Geologists discovered gold there, and news of the strike had no sooner reached the outside world than the stampede began. The Government sought for a time to stem the tide, but finally, in 1876, turned to the red owners with a demand to sell the mountains that contained the yellow metal.

The Sioux were angry. Oblivious to the solemn promises of the Treaty of 1868, the white men had invaded the northern fringes of the unceded territory, then tramped on to the reservation itself. They desecrated with mining operations the forested hills where resided the Sioux gods. At the agencies, moreover, venal agents and contractors made enormous profits from the food and clothing that had been purchased for the Indians under the terms of the treaty. Individual warriors and whole families began to slip away from the reservation to cast their lot with their kinsmen in the unceded territory to the west.

With white men swarming to the Sioux country in mounting numbers, both military and civil officials rightly concluded that peace on the northern plains could only be guaranteed by settling all Indians on the reservation, where they could be watched by agents and soldiers. Early in December 1875, therefore, the Commissioner of Indian Affairs sent out an order "to notify Sitting Bull's band and other wild and lawless Indians residing without the bounds of their reservation . . . that unless they shall remove within the bounds of their reservation (and remain there) before the 31st of January next, they shall be deemed hostile and treated accordingly by the military force." Few of the messengers bearing this order reached the remote camps before the deadline. When they did, most of the Indians scorned the demand. Dishonest agents and broken treaties had filled them with distrust and hatred of all white men.[1]

The ultimatum having failed to bring in the absentees, the Secretary of the Interior requested the Secretary of

[1] For a complete treatment of the Custer expedition of 1874, see *The Black Hills Engineer* (Custer Expedition Number), XVII, 4 (November, 1929). For data bearing on the purchase of the Black Hills, see Reports of the Secretary of the Interior, 1874, 317-18; 1875, vi-vii, 538, 686-704; 1876, 393. A concise and accurate narrative of the Black Hills difficulty is contained in E. P. Oberholtzer, *History of the United States Since the Civil War* (New York, 1926), III, 422 ff. Documentation on corruption in the Indian Service is contained in *House Reports*, 41st Cong., 3rd sess., No. 39 (1871); *ibid.*, 42nd Cong., 3rd sess., No. 98 (1873); and *House Misc. Docs.*, 44th Cong., 1st sess., No. 167 (1876).

The Background

War to bring them in by force. Brig. Gen. George Crook led 800 men north from Fort Fetterman, Wyoming, early in March. On the 16th he sent Col. J. J. Reynolds and six troops of the Third Cavalry on a rapid night march to pursue a small band of Indian hunters who were thought to be headed for a larger village. They were. At dawn on the 17th Reynolds burst into a winter camp of Cheyennes, allies of the Sioux, on the Little Powder River. Caught by surprise, the Indians scattered, but with the village in his possession Reynolds suffered an attack of timidity. The savages gained the initiative and he withdrew the command. Crook, disheartened by defeat and bitter cold, returned to Fort Fetterman to await warmer weather.

More elaborate plans, calling for three columns to converge on the hostile country, were now devised at Headquarters, Military Division of the Missouri, in Chicago. Early in April Col. John Gibbon led about 500 men of the Second Cavalry and Seventh Infantry east from Fort Ellis, Montana. Brig. Gen. Alfred H. Terry organized a second column at Fort Abraham Lincoln, on the west bank of the Missouri River opposite Bismarck, Dakota. Composed of infantry, Gatling guns, and the entire Seventh Cavalry under Custer, it numbered over 900 soldiers. Leaving Fort Lincoln on May 17, 1876, Terry and Custer struck westward for the Yellowstone. General Crook, his command reorganized, pointed north from Fort Fetterman on May 29 and marched toward the head of Rosebud Creek.

Meanwhile, the scattered bands of Sioux and Cheyennes had united. Their numbers swelled by further additions from the agencies, they moved from the Powder to the Rosebud, thence across the Wolf Mountains into the valley of a small tributary of the Little Bighorn, later known as Reno Creek. From here, a large war party under Crazy Horse went back across the Wolf Mountains. On June 17 these warriors attacked Crook's command on the Rosebud. The conflict raged back and forth across the valley throughout the afternoon, but the Sioux finally abandoned the field. Crook had used up his ammunition and had also discovered that there were a lot more hostiles than anyone dreamed. He therefore pulled back to his supply base on Goose Creek, near the present city of Sheridan, Wyoming.[2]

Unaware of Crook's withdrawal or of the unexpectedly large enemy force he had developed, Terry joined Gibbon at the confluence of Rosebud Creek and the Yellowstone River on June 21. Maj. Marcus A. Reno, returning from a scout in the valleys of the Powder, Tongue, and Rosebud, reported a hostile trail on the Rosebud leading into the Little Bighorn Valley. Terry instructed Custer to march up the Rosebud to near its headwaters, then descend the Little Bighorn from the south. Gibbon, accompanied by Terry would march his troops back up the Yellowstone and ascend the Bighorn River to the mouth of the Little Bighorn. In this

[2]The movements of the hostiles are set forth by Wooden Leg in Thomas B. Marquis, *A Warrior Who Fought Custer* (Caldwell, Ida., 1931), 155-207. For Crook's movements see John G. Bourke, *On the Border with Crook* (New York, 1891), 241-56. Bourke was a captain on Crook's staff in 1876.

manner Terry hoped to trap the hostile camp between the two forces. Much depended upon the two columns striking the Indian camp at the same time. But the camp was located only indefinitely "upon the Little Horn." On this point turned a great deal of future debate.

At noon on June 22 the Seventh Cavalry began its march up the Rosebud. As Custer wheeled to leave, Terry handed him a written copy of his instructions, the oft-quoted document that became a focal point of the Custer Controversy:[3]

> Camp at Mouth of Rosebud River
> Montana Territory
> June 22, 1876

Lieutenant-Colonel Custer
7th Cavalry

Colonel:

The Brigadier-General Commanding directs that, as soon as your regiment can be made ready for the march, you will proceed up the Rosebud in pursuit of the Indians whose trail was discovered by Major Reno a few days since. It is, of course, impossible to give you any definite instructions in regard to this movement, and were it not impossible to do so the Department Commander places too much confidence in your zeal, energy, and ability to wish to impose upon you precise orders which might hamper your action when nearly in contact with the enemy. He will, however, indicate to you his own views of what your action should be, and he desires that you should conform to them unless you shall see sufficient reason for departing from them. He thinks that you should proceed up the Rosebud until you ascertain definitely the direction in which the trail above

[3]Report of the Secretary of War, 1876, I, 462.

spoken of leads. Should it be found (as it appears almost certain that it will be found) to turn towards the Little Horn, he thinks that you should still proceed southward, perhaps as far as the headwaters of the Tongue, and then turn towards the Little Horn, feeling constantly, however, to your left, so as to preclude the escape of the Indians to the south or southeast by passing around your left flank. The column of Colonel Gibbon is now in motion for the mouth of the Big Horn. As soon as it reaches that point it will cross the Yellowstone and move up at least as far as the forks of the Big and Little Horns. Of course its future movements must be controlled by circumstances as they arise, but it is hoped that the Indians, if upon the Little Horn, may be so nearly inclosed by the two columns that their escape will be impossible.

The Department Commander desires that on your way up the Rosebud you should thoroughly examine the upper part of Tullock's Creek, and that you should endeavor to send a scout through to Colonel Gibbon's column with the information of the result of your examination. The lower part of this creek will be examined by a detachment from Colonel Gibbon's command. The supply steamer will be pushed up the Big Horn as far as the forks if the river is found to be navigable for that distance, and the Department Commander, who will accompany the column of Colonel Gibbon, desires you to report to him there not later than the expiration of the time for which your troops are rationed, unless in the mean time you receive further orders.

Very respectfully

Your obedient servant,
E. W. SMITH
Captain, 18th Infantry
Acting Assistant Adjutant General

Two days later, June 24, Custer struck a heavy Indian trail, freshly superimposed on the older trail that Major

The Background

Reno had discovered. In a series of actions that historians for years have justified, condemned, and speculated upon, he followed the trail across the Wolf Mountains. Battle was thus joined on the 25th, a day before Gibbon's scheduled arrival on the Little Bighorn.

Since the Crook fight, the Indians had moved their village from the site on Reno Creek a few miles into the Little Bighorn Valley. From a mountain peak 15 miles distant, the Crow and Ree scouts, at dawn on the 25th, detected the Sioux pony herd on the benchland west of the valley, but they were unable to convince Custer that they had located the enemy village. Confronted with unmistakable evidence of the proximity of Indians, however, Custer divided his regiment into three battalions and advanced to reconnoiter in force in an effort to find the enemy.

Three troops (H, D, and K) were assigned to Captain Benteen, three (M, A, and G) to Major Reno, and five (C, E, F, I, and L) were retained by Custer. The remaining troop (B) was detailed to guard the mule supply train and bring up the rear. Captain Benteen turned to the south and set out to scout the foothills of the Wolf Mountains, while Custer and Reno descended the valley of Reno Creek toward the Little Bighorn.

A dust cloud rising over the Little Bighorn Valley at last fixed the location of the village. But its magnitude still lay concealed by the bluffs lining the right bank of the river. Major Reno was ordered to lead his battalion (about 112 men) across the Little Bighorn to attack the village. He crossed the river and approached the upper end of the camp. Sioux warriors swarmed out to meet him. He dismounted and flung out a skirmish line. Sioux raced around the exposed left flank. He then withdrew into the timber lining a bend in the river on his right. In the tangled underbrush, the battalion fell apart, and warriors infiltrated the position. Fearing disaster, Reno assembled the command on the prairie, remounted, and led it, closely pursued by Sioux horsemen, in a desperate retreat back across the river. Only at the summit of the steep bluffs east of the river did the troopers find refuge.

The Indian hordes melted away and rode to the lower end of the village. Benteen joined Reno. He had found nothing in the rugged terrain Custer had ordered him to examine, and had come back to the main trail. He bore a message from Custer, received a few miles back, directing that the ammunition packs be brought up with haste.[4] Custer and his battalion had vanished downstream, and the sound of firing from that direction even then was heard. Capt. Thomas B. Weir, impatient over Reno's indecision, led an unauthorized sortie in the direction of the firing. Other troops followed. From a high hill to the north, they saw a dust-shrouded confusion in

[4]This famous message ("Benteen. Come on. Big village. Be quick. Bring packs. W. W. Cooke. P. S. Bring pacs.") was written by Custer's adjutant and borne to Benteen by Tptr. John Martin (Giovanni Martini). For many years it was believed to have been destroyed by a fire that razed Benteen's quarters. In 1942, however, Col. Charles Francis Bates discovered the historic scrap of paper in a private collection, and it is now in the museum at the U. S. Military Academy at West Point. See W. A. Graham, "The Lost is Found, Custer's Last Message Comes to Light," *Cavalry Journal*, LI, 4 (July-August, 1942), 60-66.

the distance, but could not make out what was taking place. Warriors appeared and drove the troops back to the first position.

The pack train had now arrived, but the troops were pinned down by fire from the growing number of Indians arriving from downriver. That night the two battalions dug in, and the following day beat off one assault after another until late in the afternoon, when the attackers withdrew. In the evening the entire village moved out of the valley to the southwest, leaving Reno's decimated battalions in possession of the hill for which they had battled for 36 hours. Next morning, June 27, the reason for the hostile exodus became apparent as the fluttering guidons of the Second Cavalry announced the approach of Terry and Gibbon from the north.

Lt. James H. Bradley, Gibbon's chief of scouts, rode in to report the discovery of 197 bodies dotting the bluffs and ravines four miles north of Reno Hill. Custer and his entire command had been wiped out. Reno's two battalions had suffered losses of 47 killed and 52 wounded.[5]

Such are the bare essentials of the Little Bighorn campaign. Every move and every word of every participant

[5]Gen. E. S. Godfrey says that, according to his memorandum book, 212 men were buried on the Custer Battlefield. The regimental returns indicate that Custer had 231 men with him. Godfrey's figures for Reno's casualties have been used, for they tally with those given by other participants. E. S. Godfrey, "Custer's Last Battle," *Century Magazine,* XLIII, 3 (January, 1892), 383. Maj. E. S. Luce, however, in his statistical compilation based on the regimental records, arrives at the figures of 32 killed and 44 wounded. E. S. Luce, *Keogh, Comanche and Custer* (p.p., St. Louis, 1939), 90 ff.

would be subjected to intensive scrutiny in the never ending effort to discover what happened on the Little Bighorn and who was to blame for the tragedy. Much of it remains speculation to this day.

Chapter II

THE PRESS

THE PRESS PLAYED AN important part in the rise of the Custer Controversy. Journalistic techniques in 1876 differed from those of today, and in the Little Bighorn "massacre" the nation's press found a subject admirably suited to emotional treatment. In the weeks after the battle, the newspapers gave full play to the sensational accounts cabled by their correspondents from the frontier. Written in lofty and impassioned prose, most were highly inaccurate. But they were eagerly devoured by a news-hungry populace and built upon by popular writers racing one another to capitalize on the interest value of the subject. Before the professional historian even entered the picture, most of the common fallacies of the Little Bighorn had been introduced and had won widespread acceptance. Besides creating these myths, the press also served as the vehicle for charge and counter-charge that initiated the long and turbulent "great debate" among the nation's military notables.

The innaccuracy of the early newspaper stories sprang largely from the limited press coverage of the Terry column. Only one correspondent went with the expedition. Mainly this resulted from a complex political imbroglio Custer had got himself into during the spring of 1876. Whether he was an innocent pawn of astute politicians who used his notoriety for partisan purposes, or a novice who tried to dabble in politics and got his fingers burned, is yet another aspect of the Custer Controversy. Suffice it to say that his activities brought down upon him the wrath of President U. S. Grant. Custer, who was to have commanded the Fort Lincoln column, led the Seventh Cavalry to Montana only because of a last-minute concession by the President. In transmitting Grant's decision, Gen. W. T. Sherman decreed that no newspapermen, "who always make trouble," could accompany Custer.

Despite this injunction, Clement A. Lounsberry, editor and publisher of the *Bismarck Tribune* and correspondent for the *New York Herald*, managed to win General Terry's permission to report the campaign. Illness in the family prevented Lounsberry from leaving Bismarck, and he sent his assistant, Mark Kellogg, in his place.[1]

1Clement A. Lounsberry, *Early History of North Dakota* (Washington, 1919), viii, 315. By contrast, the movements of Crook's column were covered by representatives of the *Chicago Times,* Chicago *Inter-Ocean, New York Herald,* and *Alta California* (San Francisco).

The Press

Kellogg faithfully sent long reports back to Bismarck to be relayed to the *New York Herald*. Shrewdly aware that the real news would probably be made by Custer, he stuck close to the Seventh's commander right up to the last fatal hour on the battlefield of the Little Bighorn. On June 29 Colonel Gibbon found his body in the ravine where C and E Troops had been slaughtered. It had been overlooked by the burial party the preceding day.[2] Thus, death prevented Kellogg from scoring what would have been one of the great beats of journalistic history. Even so, his dispatches to the *New York Herald* and his private journal on the march of the Terry column are rich source materials. Tradition has it that the journal was found intact next to his body on the Custer field. But Gibbon makes no mention of it, and it seems more likely that Kellogg left it on the supply steamer at the mouth of the Rosebud on June 21. The Kellogg notes were later elaborated by Maj. James Brisbin, Gibbon's chief of cavalry, and were brought down the river to serve as part of the lengthy dispatch that went out of Bismarck to the *New York Herald*.[3]

X   X   X

[2]John Gibbon, "Hunting Sitting Bull," *American Catholic Quarterly Review*, II, 8 (October, 1877), 699.

[3]John C. Hixon, "Custer's 'Mysterious' Mr. Kellogg," *North Dakota History*, XVII, 3 (July, 1950), 147-75. Unfortunately, that portion of Kellogg's journal subsequent to June 9 was lost some years ago. The rest, covering the first stages of the march from Fort Lincoln, has been published in Montana Historical Society, *Contributions*, IX, 1923; in several anniversary editions of the *Bismarck Tribune*; and accompanying Mr. Hixon's article. Edna Waldo (*Dakota* [Caldwell, 1936], 203) says that James Gordon Bennett, editor and publisher of the *New York Herald*, paid the daughters of Kellogg $2,000 and handsomely rewarded Major Brisbin for his efforts on behalf of the Kellogg notes.

Custer and the Great Controversy

The circumstances by which the news of the Custer Battle reached the outside world form one of the most dramatic chapters in the history of journalism. Several papers have claimed the distinction of publishing the first account. Although the *Bozeman Times,* the *Helena Herald, Helena Independent,* and *Salt Lake Tribune* all had the news in their columns by July 5, it remained for the *Bismarck Tribune* to flash the full and confirmed story to the nation.

Colonel Gibbon's command arrived at the Custer Battlefield on June 27 and spent the next two days cleaning up the field and burying the dead. The wounded of Reno's troops were prepared for a painful 15-mile journey by mule litter to the mouth of the Little Bighorn, where Grant Marsh's supply steamer, *Far West,* lay waiting to receive them aboard. On June 27 General Terry had compiled a brief report of the disaster, and on the afternoon of the 28th he summoned one of Gibbon's scouts, "Muggins" Taylor, and commissioned him to carry the dispatches through to Fort Ellis, where the news could be relayed to the East by telegraph.[4]

Taylor immediately rode northeast from the Custer Battlefield and crossed into the valley of Tullock's Creek, intending to follow that stream to Gibbon's base camp on the Yellowstone at the mouth of the Bighorn. Marauding Indians got on his trail, however, and he had to take to the hills in an effort to elude them. At dawn the next

4"Diary of Matthew Carroll," Montana Historical Society, *Contributions,* VII (Helena, 1896), 234.

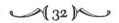

day, Taylor luckily chanced on the *Far West*, moored to the bank at the mouth of the Little Bighorn. He boarded the vessel, and as a result of his narrow escape decided to remain on the boat.

The wounded were taken aboard on the 30th, and the *Far West* steamed down the Bighorn to the Yellowstone. Here the boat tied up to await the arrival of Gibbon's command and Reno's remnant of the Seventh Cavalry, which had to be ferried across the Yellowstone before the steamer could continue down the river. Not until July 4 did the *Far West*, bearing additional dispatches, begin its 700-mile journey to Bismarck and Fort Lincoln. Taylor, however, had bidden farewell to the crew of the boat on the morning of July 1 and begun his perilous 175-mile ride to Bozeman and Fort Ellis.[5]

He rode into Stillwater on July 2, too exhausted to continue that day. He told his story to W. H. Norton, a representative of the *Helena Herald*. Norton dashed off a brief account and induced Horace Countryman, a local rancher, to carry it through to Helena.

Next day Taylor rode on to Bozeman, told his story to the editor of the *Bozeman Times*, and delivered Terry's dispatches to Capt. D. W. Benham, commanding at

[5]Joseph Mills Hanson, *Conquest of the Missouri* (2nd ed., New York, 1946), 281-303. Hanson gives the morning of June 28 as the date of Taylor's arrival at the vessel, but he is mistaken, since Taylor did not leave Terry's camp until the afternoon of the 28th. Sgt. James Wilson, Engineer Corps, who accompanied the *Far West*, noted in his diary under entry of June 29 that "Three scouts arrived during the day with the news of the disastrous battle of the Little Bighorn." Wilson's report in Report of the Secretary of War, 1877, II, 1380.

Fort Ellis. The *Times* put out an evening extra at 7 p.m. on the 3rd, but its only claim to accurate reporting lay in the statement that Custer and five companies had perished at the hands of the Sioux. Captain Benham took the official dispatches to the telegraph office in Bozeman to be relayed to Division Headquarters in Chicago, but through what Benham termed "criminal negligence" they were kept in the office until July 5 and then *mailed* to Chicago.

Meanwhile, Countryman had reached the office of the *Helena Herald* on the afternoon of July 4. Although the town was engaged in a convivial celebration of the Centennial Independence Day, Andrew J. Fiske, editor of the *Herald,* rounded up a skeleton crew and published an extra carrying Norton's story brought by Countryman. Fiske also held a commission for the Associated Press, and that evening he telegraphed the news to Salt Lake City.[6]

The *Salt Lake Tribune* carried the Fiske cable in its morning editions of July 5 and flashed the news to Chicago and New York the same day. The accounts that went out of Salt Lake City were brief and garbled, actually little more than wild rumors. Some of the eastern papers published them on July 6, although the Centennial celebration in Philadelphia was receiving most of the coverage.

[6]The accounts that appeared in the *Bozeman Times* and *Helena Herald,* together with Captain Benham's report of the telegraph office episode, are reproduced in W. A. Graham, *The Custer Myth* (Harrisburg, 1953), 349-51. The Countryman story as related by Fiske is in E. A. Brininstool, *A Trooper with Custer* (Columbus, 1926), 158-65.

The Press

The Salt Lake City reports that appeared on the morning of the 6th were generally discredited in New York and Washington. The War Department cautioned against believing them. Congress discussed the matter and concluded by assigning the whole affair to the panic of a demoralized scout who had fled in the heat of battle. The Senate passed a resolution, however, requesting information from the President, and perhaps not unrelatedly gave favorable attention to the pending bill for the transfer of responsibility for Indian affairs from the Interior to the War Department.[7]

A reporter for the *New York Herald* sought out Generals Sherman and Sheridan, both of whom were in Philadelphia. Sheridan declared that the news had arrived by a very circuitous route and had come "without any marks of credence." Sherman was in the midst of pointing out to the correspondent that the absence of any official report from the field opened the rumors to serious question when an aide handed him a note. It was the official confirmation from the field.[8]

The first reliable word of the battle had reached Division Headquarters in Chicago, from Bismarck via St. Paul, at 11 a.m. on July 6. At 3 p.m. Chief Clerk Crosby in Washington had received a wire from Col. R. C. Drum in Chicago: "Dispatches from General Terry . . . confirm the newspaper reports of a fight on the 25th of June, on the Little Horn, and of Gen. Custer's death."[9]

[7] *New York Herald,* July 7, 1876; *Senate Docs.,* 44th Cong., 1st sess., No. 81.
[8] *New York Herald,* July 7, 1876.
[9] *New York Times,* July 7, 1876.

This was the first official confirmation that the rumors were not so wild as had been supposed. It was immediately relayed to Sheridan in Philadelphia. Sheridan sent it to Sherman and it was handed to him while he was being interviewed by the *Herald* correspondent. But the *Herald* had already received the news from Clement Lounsberry in Bismarck.

✗ ✗ ✗

The steamer *Far West*, her jackstaff draped in black, docked at the Bismarck landing at 11 p.m. on the night of July 5, 54 hours and 710 miles from the mouth of the Bighorn. The crew jumped off and ran around town spreading the news. Lounsberry and the Bismarck telegraph operator, John M. Carnahan, were routed out of bed. Together with Dr. H. R. Porter, Reno's surgeon, Capt. Grant Marsh of the *Far West*, Capt. E. W. Smith of Terry's staff, and a few others from the boat, they hurried to the telegraph office. Carnahan sat down at the key and tapped out the first message, addressed to the *New York Herald*: "Bismarck, D. T., July 5, 1876:— General Custer attacked the Indians June 25, and he, with every officer and man in five companies were killed. Reno with seven companies fought in intrenched position for three days. The *Bismarck Tribune's* special correspondent was with the expedition and was killed."[10]

With Lounsberry dictating, Carnahan and his assistant, S. B. Rogers, kept the telegraph key clicking steadily

[10]*New York Herald,* July 7, 1876. The story of the drama in the telegraph office is related in Lounsberry, *Early History of North Dakota,* 316-17; and in Hanson, *Conquest of the Missouri,* 307-308. Hanson obtained his information both from Grant Marsh and from Lounsberry.

for the next 24 hours. First came Mark Kellogg's notes and Major Brisbin's commentary. Then followed interviews with Captain Smith, Dr. Porter, Captain Marsh, and Interpreter Fred Gerard. The stories of General Terry, the Crow scout Curley, some of the wounded survivors of the Reno fight, and of the death of Charley Reynolds were all obtained by Lounsberry and dictated to Carnahan. Lounsberry paused to organize some material, and Carnahan, to keep the wires open, relayed portions of the New Testament. A full list of the dead and wounded went out near dawn, and throughout the day the men in the telegraph office continued to send copy to the *Herald*. At the end of the day the story was complete. It totalled 50,000 words. James Gordon Bennett gladly paid the $3,000 in telegraph tolls that the dispatch cost him, for his paper carried by far the most comprehensive coverage of the battle.

While Lounsberry was dictating, a massive task in itself, he also found time to compose the text for his extra of the *Bismarck Tribune*. There were only two printers in town, and they had to set the type by hand, but the edition hit the streets next morning, July 6. The single word MASSACRED appeared in large block type, and the subheadings reflected the prevailing excitement: GEN. CUSTER AND 261 MEN THE VICTIMS. NO OFFICER OR MAN OF 5 COMPANIES LEFT TO TELL THE TALE. SQUAWS MUTILATE AND ROB THE DEAD. VICTIMS CAPTURED ALIVE AND TORTURED IN THE MOST FIENDISH MANNER. WHAT WILL CONGRESS DO ABOUT IT?

SHALL THIS BE THE BEGINNING OR THE END?
A four-column account of the fight, with two additional
columns listing the killed and wounded, filled the single-
sheet edition.[11]

The New York papers gave the story equally sensational treatment. Lounsberry's dispatch was not published by the *Herald* until July 7 because of a delay in
transmission at St. Paul. But his lurid accounts of savage
atrocity, together with the *Herald's* embellishments,
stirred intense excitement. The eastern populace, pre-
occupied with the Centennial observance in Philadelphia, had scarcely known that an Indian war was in
progress. Now the sudden announcement of the death
of a popular idol and every man of five troops of the
most widely known regiment in the Army struck deeply
into the public consciousness. The *Herald* reported that
the citizens of New York were profoundly shocked and
felt a keen sense of loss. Perhaps with an eye to grist
for future editorials, it eulogized the dead Custer and
declared that most New Yorkers were inclinèd to blame
the Administration's Indian policy.

Having shaken their readers with the biggest news
break of the year, the newspapers eagerly devoted column after column to reports arriving from the frontier.
The wildest rumors and grossest fabrications were
printed and· avidly read by a fascinated public. From
the papers they found their way into popular literature,
into folklore, and into history. Almost every myth of

11An original of the *Tribune Extra* for July 6, 1876 is displayed in the
Custer Battlefield Museum.

the Little Bighorn that one finds today masquerading as history may be found also in the press accounts of July 1876.

✗ ✗ ✗

In the bitter election year of 1876, the Custer tragedy dropped as from heaven into the arms of Democrats struggling against Republican campaign orators seeking to clothe them in the bloody shirt of treason and disunion. The Little Bighorn disaster, laid on a backdrop of corruption in high places and scandalous frontier fraud, instantly became a pawn on the political chessboard.

The *New York Herald* led its satellites in a vicious attack on the Administration's method of handling the Indians. On July 7 it began with an editorial denouncing President Grant as "the author of the present Indian war." Each day for several weeks the *Herald* hammered away at this theme in lengthy editorials designed to appeal to a populace outraged by the sordid procession of exposures implicating high government officials of the Grant coterie. On July 16 the paper asked, "Who Slew Custer?" In answer it declared that "The celebrated peace policy of General Grant, which feeds, clothes and takes care of their noncombatant force while the men are killing our troops—that is what killed Custer. . . . That nest of thieves, the Indian Bureau, with its thieving agents and favorites as Indian traders, and its mock humanity and pretence of piety—that is what killed Custer." The *Indianapolis Sentinel* heartily agreed that responsibility for the Indian difficulties should be placed on the President's "timid, vacillating, indecisive" policy, "with its concomitant curses of swindling agents and corrupt rings."

The Southern press sided with the anti-Grant forces. The *Mobile Register* and the *New Orleans Picayune* challenged Washington to remove United States troops from "their political services at the South and send them where the honor of the flag . . . may be redeemed. The five massacred companies of Custer attest the inhumanity and imbecility of the republican administration." The *Norfolk Landmark* favored sentencing General Terry to be "sent to the rear in company with His excellency the President," while the *Raleigh News* asserted that the Grant regime had on its hands "the blood of Custer, of Canby, of hundreds of United States soldiers."

Western journals loudly demanded a policy of extermination. The Yankton *Dakotaian* headlined its July 7 issue with CUSTER AND HIS ENTIRE COMMAND SWEPT OUT OF EXISTENCE BY THE WARDS OF THE NATION AND SPECIAL PETS OF EASTERN ORATORS. Declaring that the Indians were not men but beasts, it asked if, as winter neared, these "murdering Sioux" should be welcomed back to the agencies again to receive government charity, "bought and paid for by the brothers . . . of the men they so savagely slaughtered." The *Chicago Times* noted that "Public sentiment on the frontier demands that these outrages be punished," and the *Omaha Republican* urged the recruiting of volunteer regiments to wipe out "the whole horde of unnatural enemies of our people as they annihilated Custer's gallant 300."

Few papers rose to the defense either of the Indian or of the President. Some, however, cautioned moderation. The *New York Tribune* on July 11 scolded the partisan press for seeking political capital for the coming elections by unreasoning assaults upon Custer's superiors. "There is no reason nor any excuse for tarnishing either the memory of Custer or the reputation of Terry. Nor do the exigencies of the present political canvass call for any such cruelty or injustice." The *New York Times* also deprecated the mania for revenge and the tendency of the press to blame Grant's Peace Policy. "Whatever may have been the faults of the present administration," it said, "history will credit it with at least having made an attempt to treat the Indian fairly." But now that a prolonged war was assured, it should be prosecuted with vigor. "We must beat the Sioux, but we need not exterminate them." Support came from the old abolitionist, Wendell Phillips, who went even further. In a letter to the *Boston Transcript*, he answered the intemperate editorials with a thought-provoking question: "What kind of a war is it, where if we kill the enemy it is death; if he kills us it is a massacre?"

Within two weeks of the appearance of the first terse dispatch from Bismarck, the press had passed through two stages of its contribution to shaping the history of the Little Bighorn affair. It had spread broadcast the first distorted reports, and it had placed the "massacre" in a political context that assured its rise to a national issue of the first magnitude. It remained for the press to make its third contribution to history by serving as the forum for a battle of words among Army officers. In this it began the "great debate" that occupied the Army for over half a century.

✗　✗　✗

The press played an instrumental role in a misunderstanding that embarrassed General Terry and opened him to editorial criticism. Terry wrote two reports of the Custer Battle. In the official report, compiled at the Custer Battlefield on June 27, he merely recounted the bare facts of the movements that ended in Custer's death. By implication he shouldered the blame for failure of the campaign rather than reflect upon the dead Custer. As already related, Terry on June 28 entrusted this report to Muggins Taylor to carry through to Fort Ellis, where it could be telegraphed to Chicago by way of Salt Lake City.

On July 2, at the mouth of the Bighorn, Terry wrote a second and confidential report to Generals Sherman and Sheridan that reflected his true feelings in the matter. Beginning "I think I owe it to myself to put you more fully in possession of the facts of the late operations," Terry outlined in detail the mechanics of his plan for trapping the Sioux between the columns of Gibbon and Custer. He concluded, "I feel that our plan must have been successful had it been carried out [by Custer]." A staff officer, Capt. E. W. Smith, carried this report to Bismarck and had it wired to Chicago.

The Press

As we have seen, the June 27 report was delayed at Bozeman and then sent by regular mail to Chicago. The July 2 report reached Division Headquarters at Chicago on the 6th and was immediately telegraphed to the Division Commander, General Sheridan, in Philadelphia. Sheridan thus received the confidential report before the official report. After reading it he sent the document to General Sherman. Desiring the Secretary of War to see it, Sherman entrusted the report to a man who represented himself as a messenger but who in fact was a reporter for the *Philadelphia Enquirer.*[12] In this manner the confidential report reached the press and appeared in most dailies on July 7. The following day the June 27 report reached Washington, and as the official report was automatically released to the press, which printed it in the July 9 editions.

The publication of both reports, especially in the order in which they were received, exposed Terry to the charge of trying to arraign Custer before the nation for disobedience of explicit orders, the reverse of his intentions. The *Indianapolis Sentinel* doubtless reflected considerable opinion when on July 12 it editorialized: "The general sentiment of the country is unquestionably in refusing to coincide in General Terry's first report [the first received, but the second written], in which he made such unbecoming haste to throw the fault on the gallant

[12]Robert P. Hughes, "The Campaign Against the Sioux in 1876," *Journal of the Military Service Institution of the United States,* XVIII, 79 (January, 1896), facsimile reproduction in W. A. Graham, *The Story of the Little Big Horn* (2nd ed., Harrisburg, 1945), 18-20. Colonel Hughes was Terry's brother-in-law and his chief of staff during the 1876 campaign.

man whose life was sacrificed in the attempt to carry out his impracticable and stupidly planned campaign." Unjust though the charge may have been, the press had thrust before the public a significant question that would have been asked sooner or later anyway: Did Custer disobey orders?

Editors recognized the interest value of official opinions on where the blame should be lodged. They sent reporters far and wide to fan the flames of controversy. When queried by reporters for the Chicago papers, some of the officers at Headquarters, Military Division of the Missouri, asserted that the debacle was "brought on by that foolish pride which so often results in the defeat of men," and that "Custer, with a blind desire to eclipse Terry . . . rushed forward" into an ambuscade. A *New York Tribune* correspondent cabled from Washington that the higher army officers "agree that he [Custer] was violating orders, and say that even had he been victorious he would have been in danger of a court-martial."

For really authoritative views the newsmen turned to the country's top three soldiers: President Grant, General of the Army William T. Sherman, and Lt. Gen. Philip H. Sheridan. President Grant, interviewed by a reporter for the *New York Herald*, vehemently declared, "I regard Custer's Massacre as a sacrifice of troops, brought on by Custer himself, that was wholly unnecessary—wholly unnecessary."[13] On July 7 the

[13]*New York Herald*, Sept. 2, 1876. In evaluating the President's judgment, it is well to keep in mind his recent politically unpleasant contest with Custer in the newspapers, and the virulent attacks upon his administration by the newspapers after Custer's death.

The Press

New York Times reported that Generals Sherman and Sheridan believed Custer to have been "rashly imprudent to attack such a large number of Indians." It is interesting to note, however, that they softened the judgment considerably when it came time to prepare the War Department's Annual Report for 1876.

The press also broadcast an intemperate assault upon Custer by Gen. Samuel D. Sturgis. Sturgis was actually Colonel of the Seventh Cavalry, while Custer had been its Lieutenant Colonel. A long tour of detached service had prevented him from seeing any active duty with the regiment, and in the eyes of the people it had become identified with Custer. This, among other things, led to a mutual animosity between the two officers, and when the regiment was decimated and Sturgis' son killed, the General said some bitter things about Custer. His former subordinate, he charged, "was a brave man, but also a very selfish man. He was insanely ambitious of glory"; he was "tyrannical and had no regard for the soldiers under him"; and on the Little Bighorn he "made his attack recklessly, earlier by thirty-six hours than he should have done, and with men tired out from forced marches." Sturgis concluded on a note that suggested the real conflict between him and Custer. Contrasting his opinion of Custer with his own record before the Civil War, he added, "I never went after them that I didn't catch them." This attack upon the character and ability of a dead comrade drew the fire of pro-Custer editors. Thus placed on the defensive, Sturgis composed a further stinging indictment of Custer that promptly appeared in the papers.[14] The most charitable conclusion one can reach is that, for an officer on active duty, Sturgis' conduct demonstrated very bad taste.

In the quest for expert opinion, newsmen even approached former Confederate officers. One of James Gordon Bennett's far-ranging correspondents sought out Generals Joseph E. Johnston and John McCausland at White Sulphur Springs, West Virginia. Johnston warily sidestepped the reporter's questions; but McCausland, who had fought Custer in the Shenandoah Valley in 1864, aligned himself squarely in defense of his former opponent. McCausland said that had he been in Custer's place he would have acted in like manner. "The only way to fight with cavalry is with a dash—to charge," he declared. "I don't blame him."[15]

Another ex-Confederate who thrust himself into the debate was Gen. Thomas L. Rosser. Rosser had occupied quarters adjoining Custer's at West Point, but had resigned in 1861 to join the Confederacy. As a major general of cavalry, he had opposed Custer in numerous mounted conflicts during the Shenandoah campaign. After the war, the Virginian had secured employment with the Northern Pacific Railroad, and during the Stanley Expedition of 1873 had renewed his warm friendship with Custer. At the time of the Battle of the Little

14*St. Louis Globe-Democrat*, July 19, 1876; *New York Herald*, July 22, Aug. 13, 1876. Sturgis had an opportunity in the Nez Percé campaign to prove his ability in Indian warfare. The result was the inglorious episode at Canyon Creek, Mont. His prewar record was, however, one of which he could be justly proud.

15*New York Herald*, July 14, 1876.

Bighorn, Rosser was Division Engineer of the Northern Pacific and was living in St. Paul, Minnesota.

When an editorialist of the *St. Paul Pioneer-Press and Tribune* charged Custer with recklessness, Rosser rushed to the defense. In a letter printed by the same paper, he denied that Custer's movements had displayed recklessness and declared that the Indians would have been routed but for Reno, who "took to the hills, and abandoned Custer and his gallant comrades to their fate." This spirited defense not unexpectedly aroused the wrath of Major Reno. In a lengthy reply to Rosser, Reno reviewed the unfolding events of June 25 and concluded by calling upon Rosser to make amends and right the "wrong that was perpetrated on gallant men by your defense of Custer." But Rosser refused to change his opinions. Again he sought to clear Custer's name at the expense of Reno, ending by referring the question of guilt to General Terry as final arbiter. Intelligent and reasoned as his apologia was, Rosser after all did not have enough facts to make a sound judgment. Reno wisely let the matter drop.[16]

To the press must be assigned a large share of the responsibility for spreading the errors, myths, and legends that clutter the history of the Little Bighorn. The papers

[16]*Ibid.*, July 11 and 14, Aug. 8 and 22, 1876. Rosser later served as Chief Engineer of the Canadian Pacific Railroad. Appointed brigadier general of volunteers by President McKinley in 1898, he commanded the Second Division, First Army Corps, in the war with Spain. His division, however, got no farther than Chickamauga, Ga. Rosser died at Charlottesville, Va., in 1910. An excellent biographical sketch, emphasizing his relations with Custer, is Joseph Mills Hanson, "Thomas Lafayette Rosser," *Cavalry Journal*, Vol. 43 (March-April, 1934), 21-29.

generated intense excitement, encouraged violent denunciations of everyone from Major Reno to President Grant, and transferred the event from the military to the political arena. They thus laid the foundations for the evolution of the history of the Little Bighorn into one of the most misunderstood, confused, and controversial events of American history.

*Lt. Col. George A. Custer, Seventh Cavalry, Bvt. Maj. Gen.,
U. S. Army. Probably the last portrait taken before his death.*

—*National Archives photo, office of the Chief Signal Officer.*

Major Marcus A. Reno.

—*D. F. Barry photo, Custer Battlefield National Monument.*

Chapter III

THE GREAT DEBATE

By THE AUTUMN OF 1876, the Custer Battle had receded from the front pages of the newspapers and passed from current events to recent history. Then Frederick Whittaker of Mount Vernon, New York, plunged into the Custer Controversy. More than any single person, he kindled the Great Debate, for it was he who caused its official recognition by publishing accusations that led to the Reno Court of Inquiry.

The son of Henry and Catherine Whittaker, Frederick was born in London on December 12, 1838. His father, a solicitor, was forced to flee to America to escape imprisonment for debt when a client whose note he had endorsed defaulted. Young Frederick's training was for the law, too, but he aspired to a writing career. When the Civil War broke out, he enlisted as a private in the

Sixth New York Cavalry, was wounded in the Wilderness in May 1864, and the following February was appointed second lieutenant of Company A, New York Provisional Cavalry. Although in his later writings he invariably styled himself Captain Whittaker, there is no record of his ever having served or been brevetted in that grade.[1]

In the years after the Civil War, Whittaker's prolific pen produced scores of dime and nickel novels of the swashbuckling variety, and he became a frequent contributor to numerous popular magazines. One day he was introduced to Custer in the New York offices of *Galaxy*, a journal that was publishing the General's war memoirs and articles on plains life. Thereafter, Whittaker became a devoted admirer of the dashing cavalryman. Shortly after Custer's death, Whittaker extolled his triumphs in a eulogy that appeared in *Galaxy*, and almost immediately commenced work on a biography of his hero.[2]

Whittaker's *Life of Custer* was completed in record time and appeared on the market in December 1876. A thick, turgidly written volume, it was composed of numerous excerpts from Custer's own writings and was permeated with the influence of Mrs. Custer. It elevated the General from the ranks of ordinary mortals to a demigod whose character manifested no blemish and whose mili-

[1] Albert Johannsen, *The House of Beadle and Adams* (Norman, 1950), I, 301.

[2] Frederick Whittaker, "George Armstrong Custer," *Galaxy*, XXII, 3 (September, 1876), 362-71; Whittaker, *A Complete Life of Gen. George A. Custer* (New York, 1876).

tary record was marred by not even the slightest error of judgment.

Whittaker's treatment of the Custer Battle revealed heavy reliance upon the mass of rumor, half-truth, and fabrication that found its way into the early newspaper accounts. The novelist discounted any source not in harmony with his preconceived theories; and, although he alluded to the official reports of the participating officers, it was only to deny their charges against Custer.

Whittaker had sounded out the surviving officers of the Seventh for support in his thesis, but only one, Capt. Thomas B. Weir, had even bothered to reply. Weir shortly was assigned to recruiting duty in New York, and Whittaker promptly made his acquaintance. It seems apparent, however, that when the persistent writer badgered Weir to sign an affidavit containing specific allegations against Reno, Weir refused. The relationship soon ended with the Captain's untimely death in December 1876.[3]

As have many of his disciples since, Whittaker construed Terry's orders to Custer as merely setting forth a guide to be followed unless circumstances dictated otherwise. They were, he said, "entirely advisory and permissory, *not peremptory.*" He seized upon the clause stating that "the Department Commander places too

[3]Whittaker never mentioned Weir by name. A sarcastic recital of the Whittaker-Weir story, together with a scathing indictment of Whittaker's methods, was contained in a letter published by the *Philadelphia Times,* March 13, 1879. The letter was written by one Robert Newton Price of Philadelphia, and was inspired by Captain Benteen. Benteen was annoyed by a Whittaker missive appearing in the *New York Sun,* Feb. 26, 1879. These newspaper articles, and Benteen's letter to Price, are reprinted in Graham, *Custer Myth,* 325-32.

much confidence in your zeal, energy and ability to wish to impose upon you precise orders which might hamper your action when nearly in contact with the enemy," but "desires that you conform to them [the orders] unless you shall see sufficient reason for departing from them." This clause, Whittaker contended, proved that "Custer cannot be held legally or morally responsible for any departure from Terry's advice," for "the whole matter is left entirely in his discretion."

Reno was arraigned for having failed to push his attack on the upper end of the Sioux village as ordered by Custer. He became demoralized and, instead of hugging the timber and trusting to Custer to come to his support, retreated to the bluffs. As a result, the Indians broke loose from the fight at the upper end of the camp and concentrated against Custer at the lower end. But Benteen's offense was worse yet, for, alleged Whittaker, he was guilty of willful disobedience. Upon receipt of Custer's urgent instructions to march forward quickly with the pack train ("Come on. Big Village. Be Quick. Bring Packs."), he obeyed by "advancing three miles in two hours, and joining Reno in a three hours' halt," by which time it was too late to help Custer.

These charges were indeed serious. But Whittaker did not rest his case here. He concluded by leveling an undiluted charge of cowardice at Major Reno, and strongly urged the convening of a court of inquiry empowered to call forth testimony of participants and decide whether or not his conclusions were correct. "The nation demands such a court, to vindicate the name of a dead hero from the pitiless malignity, which first slew him and then pursued him beyond the grave."

The reaction was not long in coming, especially in professional circles. The *Army and Navy Journal,* of which Whittaker himself was an official, on December 23 took exception to his historical method. "To indiscriminately laud your hero is undoubtedly the easiest way of writing a biography," it editorialized, "and there is much excuse for it in the case of a work rushed into print to catch the fleeting tide of popular interest. It is questionable, however, whether the subject of the eulogy gains or loses most by such partisanship." The columns of this periodical were heavy during 1877 with outraged protests of officers whose military record Whittaker had stained in his attempt to paint a flawless portrait of his hero at the expense of all who, at one time or another, had chanced to cross Custer's path.

More scholarly sights were drawn on the book by James Joseph Talbot, writing in the *Penn Monthly.* His appraisal of Whittaker's biographical ineptitude probably could not be improved today:

> Capt. Whittaker is not qualified to express an intelligent or impartial opinion upon the subject of the last battle, for two very good reasons: First, he had to rely upon the conflicting and unreliable newspaper reports published at the time . . . for his information upon the subject, [and] it is impossible, under these circumstances, . . . to form a just conclusion upon the subject. Second, he is prejudiced in favor of his hero, in his self-appointed task of apotheosizing him at the expense of every one else, living or dead, and therefore can see no wrong in anything he did, and no

right in anything anyone else did if it conflicted with his hero's interest.[4]

The importance of Whittaker's *Life of Custer* in shaping the public image of Custer and the Battle of the Little Bighorn can hardly be exaggerated. In the field of popular literature, book after book appeared in the 1880's and 1890's that leaned heavily upon his interpretations. In many he is the sole source consulted. In a number he is flagrantly plagiarized.

✗　✗　✗

Some authorities have charged that Whittaker's fight for a court of inquiry was motivated by a desire to stimulate lagging sales of his Custer biography. Whether inspired by a genuine wish to clear Custer's name or by more commercial motives, he tried to provoke the War Department into ordering an official investigation of Reno's conduct in the battle. Failing in this attempt, he turned his attention to Congress. On May 18, 1878, he addressed a lengthy letter to W. W. Corlett, Delegate from Wyoming Territory. In this letter, Whittaker accused Reno of "gross cowardice" in failing to push a vigorous attack on the upper end of the Sioux camp, and later, when firing was heard from down the river, in failing to cut through to Custer's aid. In conclusion, Whittaker urged Corlett to seek authorization for a court in order that the charges could be examined.[5]

[4] James Joseph Talbot, "Custer's Last Battle," *Penn Monthly*, XIII, 93 (September, 1877), 679-99.

[5] W. A. Graham (ed.), *The Official Record of a Court of Inquiry Convened . . . Upon the Request of Major Marcus A. Reno . . .* (Pacific Palisades, Calif., 1951), iii-iv. Hereafter *Reno Court of Inquiry.*

The Great Debate

Corlett introduced the petition in the House of Representatives on June 8, 1878. Referred to the Committee on Military Affairs, it was reported favorably on June 12 but died when Congress adjourned without taking action. Then Reno himself appealed to President Rutherford B. Hayes for a court of inquiry to investigate Whittaker's allegations, "that the many rumors started by camp gossip may be set at rest and the truth made fully known."[6] Whittaker later observed that Reno was extremely shrewd in waiting until the two-year statute of limitations had expired before asking for an investigation.[7]

The Reno Court of Inquiry convened at Chicago's Palmer House on January 13, 1879. Three distinguished officers composed the Court: Col. John H. King, Ninth Infantry, President; Col. Wesley Merritt, Fifth Cavalry; and Lt. Col. W. B. Royall, Third Cavalry. These men were not charged with judging guilt or innocence. That is the function of a court-martial. A court of inquiry is merely an investigating body that determines whether the evidence warrants further proceedings. First Lt. Jesse M. Lee, Ninth Infantry, served as Recorder, mili-

[6]*Ibid.; Cong. Rec.,* 45th Cong., 2nd sess., 4374. Major Reno at this time was living in Harrisburg, Pa., undergoing a two-year suspension from duty. Accused of using his official position as post commander at Fort Abercrombie, Dak., to take personal revenge upon the wife of a subordinate officer, he was tried by court-martial in St. Paul in the spring of 1877. The court found him guilty of conduct unbecoming an officer and gentleman and condemned him to dismissal. The sentence was mitigated by order of the President, Rutherford B. Hayes, to suspension from rank and pay for two years. *Senate Docs.,* 47th Cong., 2nd sess., No. 926.

[7]*New York Sun,* Feb. 26, 1879.

tary counterpart of prosecutor. Reno was ably defended by civilian counsel, Lyman D. Gilbert, Assistant Attorney General of Pennsylvania.

Cavalrymen decked in full dress flooded the Palmer House and set the chamber maids agog. The city took great interest in the proceedings, and the newspapers recounted minute details of the spectacle. In the heavy prose of the day, *Times* and *Tribune* writers described the appearance and actions of each officer. At first the Court would not permit the newsmen to record the testimony, but finally relented when they developed an ingenious system of relays: one man sat for a few minutes committing testimony to memory as it was given, then another took his place while the first dashed out to scribble down the testimony from memory.

Lieutenant Lee opened by requesting the presence of Frederick Whittaker. Over Reno's strenuous objection, the Court authorized his summons. Within a week the indomitable novelist appeared on the scene and promptly favored the press with a statement.[8] He was not satisfied, he declared, with the "scope of the present inquiry and the orders by which the court is limited." He alluded mysteriously to "private letters from Washington" that assured him a trial by the United States Senate—another scheme destined to frustration. As a matter of justice, he added, he wished to set the record straight by exonerating Captain Benteen of the accusation, contained in the *Life of Custer*, of disobedience of Custer's orders to hurry forward with the pack train. Since arriving in

[8]*Chicago Times,* Jan. 13, 1879; *New York Times,* Jan. 24, 1879.

The Great Debate

Chicago, Whittaker had talked with Trumpeter John Martin, who carried the famous last message from Custer, and was now convinced that he had done Benteen a grievous wrong. One can imagine Benteen's wintry smile when he read this in the papers.

The newspaper statement was the limit of Whittaker's contribution to the Reno Court of Inquiry. He had no legally admissible evidence, and the Court would not permit him to examine witnesses. Consequently, he was forced to content himself with sending in an occasional question for Recorder Lee to put to a witness.

The hearings lasted four weeks. Twenty-three witnesses testified, including all but three of the officers who had fought under Reno on the bluffs.[9] As they trooped on the stand to submit to Lee's gentle prodding and Gilbert's adroit cross-examination, a sharp difference of opinion emerged. Most of the officers either endorsed Reno's actions or manifested a decided reluc-

---

[9]Witnesses: Capt. F. W. Benteen; B. F. Churchill, civilian packer; Sgt. F. A. Culbertson; Sgt. Edward Davern; Lt. C. C. DeRudio; Lt. W. S. Edgerly; John Frett, civilian packer; Col. John Gibbon, Seventh Infantry; F. F. Gerard, civilian interpreter; Capt. E. S. Godfrey; Lt. L. R. Hare; George Herendeen, civilian scout; Lt. Edward Maguire, Engineer Corps; Tptr. John Martin (Giovanni Martini); Capt. E. G. Mathey; Capt. Myles Moylan; Capt. T. M. McDougall; Capt. J. S. Payne, Fifth Cavalry; Surgeon H. R. Porter; Maj. M. A. Reno; Lt. Col. M. V. Sheridan, military secretary to the Lieutenant General; Lt. C. A. Varnum; and Lt. G. D. Wallace.

Absent: Capt. T. H. French, undergoing court-martial at Fort Lincoln, Dak.; Capt. T. B. Weir, who died in December 1876; and Lt. F. M. Gibson. French was interviewed at Bismarck on Jan. 18, 1879. He said that he had not seen Major Reno from the evening of the 25th until noon on the 26th and could find no one that did, "in other words," said the newspaper, "that Reno slunk away in a hole and left the command to Benteen." *New York Times,* Jan. 19, 1879.

tance to criticize them. Only Capt. E. S. Godfrey reflected upon Reno's fortitude, and that mildly. He described the Major's demeanor as one of "nervous timidity," and observed that Captain Benteen seemed to be exercising the functions of commanding officer to a greater extent than Reno.

The civilians, however, were not so reticent. Dr. Porter, Fred Gerard, and the civilian packers denounced Reno in harsh terms. Porter painted a picture of confusion and demoralization among the command during the flight from the valley to the bluffs. He too believed Benteen in reality had exercised command. Gerard, who had been left in the timber by the rapid retirement of the troops, was not inclined to be generous toward the Major. Gilbert bore hard on Gerard, and by dwelling upon his "marriage" to an Indian woman—a common enough arrangement on the frontier—sought to discredit him in the eyes of the three colonels.

Interest revived when B. F. Churchill, a civilian packer, testified that Reno had been drunk on the night of June 25 and had engaged in an altercation with another packer, John Frett. Frett was hurried to the stand to enlarge upon the incident. Gilbert swung into a vigorous counter-attack. Failing to shake Churchill and Frett in their stories, he paraded a line of officers on the stand to swear that they had observed no signs of intoxication in Reno at any time during the engagement.[10]

[10]This question has been a subject of debate at various times since raised at the Inquiry. According to an article in the *Northwestern Christian Advocate.* Sept. 7, 1904, Reno admitted to the *Advocate's* editor, Rev. Arthur Edwards,

The Great Debate

On February 9 the examination at last drew to a close. On the 10th Gilbert delivered the summation of Reno's case. On the 11th Lieutenant Lee made his closing remarks, and the members of the Court retired to consider the voluminous evidence accumulated during the month-long hearing.[11] Despite press speculation that the Court would recommend further and more definitive trial of Major Reno,[12] the opinion of the three officers, as handed down on February 13, declared that "while subordinates in some instances did more for the safety of the command . . . than did Major Reno there was nothing in his conduct which requires animadversion from this Court," and that "no further proceedings are necessary."

The official opinion failed to clear Reno's name in many unofficial quarters. In view of the sharp difference between the testimony of the officers and the civilians, the suspicion lingered that the Army had closed ranks to protect its own, the officers, for reasons of unit pride or military politics, declining to express their true feelings. On the other hand, it was shown that each of the civilian witnesses had his own personal quarrel with Reno, and had nothing to lose by using the Court as a

that his behavior in the engagement had been influenced by alcohol. Most historians, however, balance this against the substantial testimony to the contrary developed by the Inquiry and acquit Reno of the charge.

[11] Among the exhibits attached to the evidence was a petition signed by 236 enlisted men of the Seventh Cavalry immediately following the battle. It praised the courage of Reno and Benteen and requested their elevation in rank, Reno to lieutenant colonel vice Custer killed, Benteen to major vice Reno promoted. The petition was denied, however, because promotions had already been made on the basis of seniority.

[12] *New York Times*, Feb. 11, 1879.

means of pursuing it. Human motivation being what it is, it is probable that both interpretations contain a seed of truth, and that the soundest interpretation lies somewhere between the two extremes.

Whatever the answer, the chief value of the Reno Court of Inquiry resides not in its opinion, but in the mass of first-hand source material it consigned to future historians. Seldom does the historian encounter a past event for which so many participants have left detailed accounts, and it is one of the ironies of history that, with such a mountain of evidence, the Battle of the Little Bighorn remains cloaked in mystery.

Actually, little use was made of the testimony until about 1920. The official transcript promptly got locked away in the War Department under a restricted classification. Although the unofficial transcript was available to any researcher who cared to consult the files of the *Chicago Times*, few did so. After World War I, Col. W. A. Graham, an officer on the staff of the Judge Advocate General in Washington, developed an intense interest in the history of the Custer Fight, and because of this interest became a sort of unofficial custodian of the record. In 1921 he made an abstract of the testimony, and used it in writing *The Story of the Little Big Horn*, published in 1926. The Colonel furnished copies of the abstract to Secretary of War Newton D. Baker, Generals Nelson A. Miles, Edward S. Godfrey, and Hugh L. Scott; to writers E. A. Brininstool and W. M. Camp; and later Frederick F. Van de Water, author of *Glory Hunter*.[13] The abstract

---

13Graham to author, Dec. 13, 1951.

was published by the Stackpole Company in September 1954, one month before Colonel Graham's death. Meanwhile, the complete record had been transferred to the National Archives in 1941, and in 1951 Colonel Graham succeeded in having the restricted classification lifted. The same year he published, by direct liquid duplication process, a limited edition of 125 copies.

Having won official vindication, Reno returned to the regiment in the spring of 1879. The following autumn he got involved in a barroom brawl, among other things, and was brought before a court-martial, which sentenced him to dismissal from the Service. Undergoing treatment for a tongue cancer brought on by excessive smoking, he died at Providence Hospital in Washington, D. C., on March 1, 1889.[14]

A manuscript found among his effects contained Reno's last word on the Custer Battle. The battle, he said, had been lost because of "several great blunders": Custer's disobedience of orders, his division of the regiment without proper reconnaissance, and the exhausted condition of his command—all stemming from a driving ambition on the part of Custer. The manuscript closed on a note that doubtless betrayed something of the ordeal that Reno had lived through since the battle: "Even now, after the lapse of nearly ten years, the horror of Custer's battlefield is still vividly before me, and the harrowing sight of those mutilated and decomposing bodies crown-

---

[14]*Senate Reports*, 47th Cong., 2nd sess., No. 926; *Army and Navy Journal*, April 6, 1889.

ing the heights on which poor Custer fell will linger in my memory till death."[15]

Frederick Whittaker continued to turn out dime novels, at the same time embracing spiritualism with a fervor approaching insanity. He grew increasingly eccentric and often displayed fits of violent irascibility. His suspicious nature caused him to carry a pistol as a regular habit. On May 13, 1889, he caught his cane in the stair railing of his home and fell down the steps. The pistol went off and the bullet fatally wounded him in the head. Thus passed from the scene, hardly a month after the death of Reno, he whom the press had heralded as "Major Reno's prosecutor."[16]

✕   ✕   ✕

A year and a half after the death of Whittaker and Reno, Gen. Alfred H. Terry passed away. A highly respected and beloved officer, the "Hero of Fort Fisher" was buried at New Haven, Connecticut, on December 19, 1890. The Rev. Dr. Theodore T. Munger, distinguished Congregational clergyman and well-known author, officiated at the services. During the funeral oration, Dr. Munger made the following assertion:

> General Terry never came under accusation but he did not wholly escape a kind of subdued and qualified criticism in connection with the Custer affair in 1876. It was inevitable that blame for the terrible but magnificent blunder should rest somewhere, and naturally upon the officer in

[15]Reproduced in Frazier and Robert Hunt, *I Fought with Custer* (New York, 1947), 164.

[16]Johannsen, *House of Beadle and Adams*, 301-302.

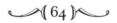

The Great Debate

command, whose subordinates are supposed to carry out his orders. That Custer should have fallen into such a trap would naturally reflect upon his superiors. The facts in the case have never been generally known. It is permitted me to speak of them today without reserve, and I do so because General Terry's conduct in the matter seems to me to be the noblest act in his life and the truest index of his character. Custer's fatal movement was in direct violation of both verbal and written orders. When his rashness ended in the total destruction of his command General Terry withheld the fact of the disobedience of orders, and suffered an imputation hurtful to his military reputation to rest upon himself rather than subject a brave but indiscreet subordinate to a charge of disobedience.[17]

Dr. Munger's judgment, delivered as truth with no allowance for differing interpretations, touched off a chain reaction of argument extending well into the 20th century. Gen. James B. Fry, then on the retired list, took up the cudgel. The *Century Magazine* for January 1892 published a lengthy article by Capt. Edward S. Godfrey, who had been a lieutenant commanding Troop K during Reno's fight for the bluffs. Entitled "Custer's Last Battle," it was a temperate defense of Custer's actions. Not so moderate, however, were the appended remarks, in several pages of fine print, by General Fry.[18]

[17]Reproduced in James G. Wilson, "Two Modern Knights Errant," *The Cosmopolitan*, XI, 3 (July, 1891), 302, note.

[18]James B. Fry, "Comments by General Fry on the Custer Battle," *Century Magazine*, XLIII, 3 (January, 1892), 385-87. Fry graduated from West Point in 1847, served as Provost Marshal General during the Civil War, and in the Adjutant General's Department on the staffs of Generals Sheridan, Halleck, and Hancock from 1866 to 1881. He retired on July 1, 1881, with the regular rank of colonel and a brevet of major general. An author of note, he is credited

Fry came out squarely in defense of Custer. He charged that "it is highly probable that [Terry's] plan when Custer moved had neither the force nor importance which it subsequently acquired in Terry's mind." Furthermore, it was based upon a faulty estimate of enemy strength, and could not have succeeded even had Custer tried to carry it out. If Custer was strong enough to continue on up the Rosebud, as contemplated in the orders, and wait to be attacked, as Crook had been a week earlier, he was certainly strong enough to make the attack himself. From this questionable analysis, Fry concluded that

> The order Custer received was to proceed up the Rosebud in pursuit of the Indians. Surely he did not disobey that. Everything else was left to his discretion. ["It is, of-course, impossible to give you any definite instructions in regard to this movement, and were it not impossible to do so the Department Commander places too much confidence in your zeal, energy and ability to wish to impose upon you precise orders which might hamper your action when nearly in contact with the enemy, and found it·impossible to give] Terry did not wish to hamper Custer's actions when nearly in contact with the enemy, and I found it impossible to give him precise orders, plainly Custer did not, could not, disobey orders in any blamable sense, and plainly, also, he was expected to come "in contact with the enemy."

Fry had written to Rev. Munger to learn the source of his indictment of "one dead soldier at the Christian burial of another." Munger had given the name of Col.

with a large number of publications in a variety of fields. He died on July 11, 1894. F. B. Heitman, *Historical Register and Dictionary of the U. S. Army* (Washington, 1903), I, 439; *Army and Navy Journal*, July 11, 1881.

The Great Debate

Robert P. Hughes, Terry's brother-in-law and aide-de-camp in the 1876 campaign. "Colonel Hughes . . . admits that he was the source of Dr. Munger's information. Called upon more than once, he fails to produce or specify any orders disobeyed by Custer. Indeed there can be no such orders."[19]

While Hughes was drafting a rebuttal to Fry, Gen. James Brisbin, Gibbon's cavalry chief in 1876, addressed a caustic letter to Godfrey. Alluding to Fry's dissertation, he asked, "Now what does old Fry know about the battle of the Little Big Horn? Only what he has read and nothing more . . . and it is absurd for him to write about what he knows nothing of . . . I presume there has been nothing since the birth of Christ that old Fry does not think he knows all about it."[20]

Meanwhile, Colonel Hughes had delved into the official records and come up with a rejoinder to Fry's imputations against kinsman Terry. After some delay, he submitted the finished product to *Century*. That journal, however, would agree to publish it only if Hughes pared it to the length of Fry's commentary. Since Godfrey's monograph had provided a solid foundation for Fry's

[19]Col. R. P. Hughes rose from the volunteer ranks to brevet colonel during the Civil War and was appointed captain in the 18th U. S. Infantry in 1866. He served for many years on General Terry's staff. At the time of the debate with Fry he was a colonel in the Inspector General's Department. Hughes served as a brigadier general of volunteers in the war with Spain, retired a major general in 1903, and died in 1909. Heitman, *Dictionary of the U. S. Army*, I, 552.

[20]Brisbin to Godfrey, Jan. 1, 1892. Unpublished manuscript copy in Monroe, Mich., Public Library. The letter was reproduced in E. A. Brininstool's *Troopers with Custer* in 1952 but with some of Brisbin's picturesque old-school language deleted. Brisbin died within a month after writing this letter.

remarks, Hughes did not feel that an adequate reply could be compressed into such a brief space. As a result, he decided to wait and see what effect the Fry-Godfrey discourse would have.

The effect became apparent in 1895, when *Scribner's Magazine* published serially "A History of the Last Quarter-Century in the United States." The author was Dr. E. Benjamin Andrews, President of Brown University, later Chancellor of the University of Nebraska. In his treatment of the Custer disaster, Dr. Andrews followed Godfrey's interpretations. He dismissed the question of disobedience of orders, stating that "some of General Terry's friends charged Custer with transgressing his orders in fighting as he did. This has been disproved."[21]

This generalization angered Hughes. He wrote to the Doctor asking to know the evidence upon which he had based his exoneration of Custer. Andrews replied that Godfrey and Fry had been his authority. Hughes thereupon resurrected the manuscript that *Century* had rejected. He submitted it to the *Journal of the Military Service Institution of the United States*. The *Journal* was a publication of limited circulation, chiefly among military men, so Hughes' rebuttal attracted little attention outside professional circles.[22]

Colonel Hughes admitted that he had been the source of Doctor Munger's remarks at Terry's funeral, but he

[21] E. Benjamin Andrews, "A History of the Last Quarter-Century in the United States," *Scribner's Magazine*, XVIII, 6 (June, 1895), 732-33.

[22] See Ch. 2, note 12, p. 43, for full citation.

denied authorizing their use in the funeral oration. None-theless, the allegations were "fully warranted by the facts," and Hughes set out to prove that Custer disobeyed mandatory orders by following the hostile trail and precipitating battle when and where he did.

When Custer marched up the Rosebud, alleged Hughes, he was supposed to follow that stream past the point where the trail was known, as a result of Reno's scout, to cross to the Little Bighorn. He was in fact expected to march nearly to the head of the Rosebud before dropping down the Little Bighorn on June 26. This would give the slower moving infantry time to complete its longer journey and be in a position, on the 26th, to cooperate with the Seventh Cavalry. The Indian trail in truth was found to cross to the Little Bighorn. Terry's anticipations had been confirmed. Custer was therefore not justified in departing from the plan of action.

Gibbon's command was sighted by the Indians just when Terry had predicted. Had Custer continued up the Rosebud, argued Hughes, he would have consumed the required time and descended the valley against the encampment as Gibbon pressed it from the north. Had Custer adhered to the plan, asked Hughes, "is it too much to believe that one of the most brilliant victories over the Indians would have been won?"

Fry, however, had argued that Terry, by shading his orders with a permissive tone, in effect recognized the necessity for a flexible tactical plan, allowing for unforeseen circumstances. This was why he inserted the clause admitting the impracticability of giving precise instruc-

Custer and the Great Controversy

tions. Colonel Hughes, on the other hand, declared that courtesy of phraseology detracts nothing from the binding character of military orders, and he emphasized that General Terry was distinguished by a singular kindheartedness that made inclusion of the "escape clause" only natural. He called attention to the sentence following the escape clause, which bound Custer to adhere to Terry's "suggestions" unless he saw "sufficient reason for departing from them." Hughes believed that his construction of Terry's plan of action, considered in light of the situation as it in fact developed, demonstrated that sufficient reason did not exist.[23]

Thus, having skillfully led his readers to the conclusion that Terry's plan in conception was flawless, in execution

[23]Dr. Charles Kuhlman (*Legend into History*) took exception with Colonel Hughes' reasoning. He argued that, since Major Reno's discovery of the hostile trail, a large band of Indians has passed over it. When Custer struck the trail, therefore, it evidenced a freshness that indicated the proximity of the village, and in numbers unexpectedly large. Kuhlman shows that Hughes and other Terry partisans suppressed or distorted the fact that the "general impression" on June 21 was that the hostiles were on the *upper reaches* of the Little Bighorn. But Custer was now confronted by a trail so fresh that his quarry could be no more than 30 miles distant. It consequently became a matter of urgency to locate the village and ascertain its true strength. This, maintains Kuhlman, was the "sufficient reason." He further shows that the Indians had in fact intended to move up the Little Bighorn, but reports of an antelope herd near the mouth of the Little Bighorn caused them to change their minds. Thus, even as Custer attacked the village on June 25, the squaws had begun the task of dismantling the tepees for the move down the valley. Kuhlman points out that, had Custer gone on up the Rosebud, the Indians would have moved their village to the mouth of the Little Bighorn on the 25th. History might indeed have been written differently, maintains Kuhlman, for Terry and Brisbin arrived at the mouth of the Little Bighorn shortly before dawn on the 26th. They had with them only four troops of cavalry exhausted by an all-night march. The infantry was still lost in the badlands along the Bighorn. Kuhlman's thesis, needless to say, has found its challengers.

destroyed by the precipitate action of a glory-hunter, Hughes concluded:

> I have been thoroughly conversant all these years with the noble and generous sacrifice, the complete abnegation of self that General Terry knowingly made for the avowed purpose of shielding a dead man from public blame. I have seen him receive thrust after thrust, year after year, on this matter, and quietly ignore it with some such remark as "Blinder Eifer Shadet nur." But when this striking example of his main characteristic was cited in his praise at his bier, and I find the facts denied, the sacrifice and consequent suffering scoffed at, and the magnanimous man himself arrogantly and ignorantly criticized and adroitly belittled, both as man and soldier, it becomes a duty to expose facts enough to meet the case.

Doctor Andrews' retort came the following year. In 1896 his series of articles was consolidated in book form. Taking note of Hughes' monograph, he observed that this officer "seemed to the present writer not at all to justify his views." He then ably developed a rebuttal that marshaled his own powers of logic against Hughes' interpretations.[24]

Four years later another eminent Army officer cast his lot with the Custerphiles. In his autobiography, Gen. George A. Forsyth, hero of Beecher's Island, set forth his views on the controversy.[25] He conceded that Terry's

[24]E. Benjamin Andrews, *The History of the Last Quarter-Century in the United States*, 1870-1895 (2 v., New York, 1896), I, 191.

[25]George A. Forsyth, *The Story of a Soldier* (New York, 1900), 322 *et seq.* Forsyth entered the Army as a private in the Chicago Dragoons in 1861 and rose through the ranks of Illinois cavalry to brigadier general of volunteers. In 1868 he recruited a company of frontiersmen for Indian service on the southern plains. This unit valiantly withstood a four-day siege, conducted by Roman Nose

plan, when conceived, contemplated that the Seventh Cavalry should not follow the hostile trail when struck, but continue up the Rosebud before turning to the Little Bighorn. But, he observed with reference to the escape clause, "the written instructions given General Custer gave him great latitude."

Forsyth's logic ran like this: Custer's orders permitted him to exercise his own discretion in attacking the hostiles. His regiment numbered 700, while Sitting Bull, if reports of the Indian Bureau were correct, could muster a maximum of 1,000 men. It was almost certain that the proximity of soldiers had been detected by the Indians and that any delay would permit Sitting Bull to flee before Terry's trap could be sprung. Custer was then "nearly in contact with the enemy."

"Under the peculiar conditions of affairs," continued Forsyth, "bearing in mind the only information he could possibly have concerning Sitting Bull's forces, was Custer justified, in a military sense and within the scope of his orders, in making the attack? In the opinion of the writer, he was within his orders and fully justified from a military standpoint in so doing."

✗   ✗   ✗

In 1896 Maj Gen Nelson A. Miles, Commanding General of the Army, added a new dimension to the Custer Controversy. Actually, he had been an ardent participant

and other hostile chiefs, on an island in the Arikara Fork of the Republican River. From 1869 to 1873 he was lieutenant colonel and military secretary to Lieutenant General Sheridan and from 1878 to 1881 aide-de-camp to Sheridan. He served as Lieutenant Colonel of the Fourth Cavalry from 1881 until his retirement in 1890. Heitman, *Dictionary of the U. S. Army*, I, 430.

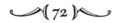

for many years, and his views were well known. He believed that Custer had acted correctly in following the hostile trail into the Little Bighorn Valley, and that he and his five troops had been sacrificed by the timidity of Major Reno. General Miles spoke from the pinnacle of the military pyramid, and had plenty of experience to add authority to his pronouncements. But he also had an unfortunate habit of building his case on expansive generalities—as Colonel Graham styled it, of talking *ex cathedra*. In knowledgeable circles, this tended to weaken his arguments.

In 1896 Miles published a large and handsomely illustrated volume of reminiscences of military experiences in the Civil and Indian wars.[26] His treatment of the Custer Fight followed his familiar line of argument, but in addition he related a tale that sparked a long and, for historians, very productive dispute. He had in his possession, he wrote, an affidavit containing the testimony of "the last witness who heard the two officers [Terry and Custer] in conversation together the night before the commands separated." The anonymous affiant alleged that on the night of June 21, presumably

[26]Nelson A. Miles, *Personal Recollections and Observations of Nelson A. Miles* (Chicago, 1896). Miles was born on Aug. 8, 1839 (four months before Custer). During the Civil War he rose rapidly from second lieutenant of Massachusetts Volunteers to major general commanding Grant's V Army Corps. As Colonel of the Fifth Infantry on the frontier, he distinguished himself in the campaigns against the Kiowas and Comanches (1874-75), the Sioux and Cheyennes (1876-81), the Nez Percés (1877), and the Apaches (1886). He was promoted to major general in the Regular Army in 1890, commanded the Army during the Spanish-American War, and was elevated to Lieutenant General in 1900, retiring in 1903. Miles married the niece of General Sherman and Senator John Sherman of Ohio. He died in 1925.

after the conference on the *Far West*, the following conversation took place:

Terry: "Custer, I don't know what to say for the last."

Custer: "Say whatever you want to say."

Terry: "Use your own judgment and do what you think best if you strike the trail. And whatever you do, Custer, hold on to your wounded."

The affidavit story stirred up the Custerphobes, for if Terry really did say "Use your own judgment and do what you think best if you strike the trail," the case against Custer for disobedience of orders collapses. Further historical prosecution of Custer depended upon exposing the affidavit as fraudulent; further defense upon verifying its authenticity. Only Miles could supply the answer, and he was not accustomed to having his word questioned.

In 1904 Dr. Cyrus Townsend Brady, clergyman-author whose pen produced many popular histories, published *Indian Fights and Fighters*. With Dr. Brady acting as a kind of historical interlocutor, and the appendix of his book serving as the forum of discussion, a lively debate was developed between the principals in the military controversy. General Fry had died, but included were contributions from Generals Godfrey, Hughes, Henry B. Carrington, Charles A. Woodruff, and in a rather negative fashion, General Miles.

Brady addressed several inquiries to Miles in an attempt to find out the circumstances surrounding the affidavit and the name of the affiant. When Miles finally replied, he confined himself to an evasive and rather pompous discourse, the sense of which was that Custer did not disobey orders simply because General Miles said that he did not. Brady persisted, but met with icy silence. The General was not talking. An intelligent marshaling of arguments followed. General Hughes stated that "It is not a new experience to learn that the views of General Miles and myself are at variance. Indeed, it seems that they are never in accord." (This was not so brave as might seem, for Miles had retired from active service.) He too, said Hughes, had challenged Miles to produce the mysterious affidavit, only to be rebuffed. Hughes discredited the whole story, but he could offer no proof that it was false. He observed, however, that to caution a subordinate on so elemental a maxim as holding on to his wounded would have been an insult and breach of military etiquette of which Terry was wholly incapable.

General Godfrey submitted a scholarly treatise defending Custer, but professed to know nothing of the affidavit. He was willing to accept Hughes' judgment, he said. General Carrington, of Fort Phil Kearny fame,[27] had nothing of value to contribute. But General Woodruff, who had been a subaltern with Gibbon in 1876, ridiculed Miles' story and concluded that if Custer did not violate orders, "I don't see how it is possible for the charge of disobedience of orders to hold against any

[27]Carrington was the center of a controversy himself. Commanding Fort Phil Kearny in 1866, he was accused of fault in the annihilation of Capt. William J. Fetterman and 80 soldiers by Red Cloud's Sioux on Dec. 21, 1866. Superior officers hastily removed him from command, and he spent many years in an effort, eventually partially successful, to clear his name.

man, under any circumstances, when away from his superiors."

Despite the almost unanimous implication that the affidavit was an adroitly fabricated instrument of Custer partisanship, Miles was not visibly perturbed by the polemics. Seven years later, in 1911, he published a revision and condensation of *Personal Recollections*. Again he related the affidavit story, this time with two additions made necessary by the letters to Brady. Though alluding to the debate in Brady's book only by indirection, Miles named the affiant as "General Custer's servant." To counter Hughes' assertion that Terry would not have affronted a subordinate by reminding him to hold on to his wounded, Miles added, "It will be remembered that not long before . . . it was charged that a command had left its wounded to the mercy of the Indians."[28]

A decade later Col. W. A. Graham succeeded in dispelling some of the mystery. In the early 1920's, while collecting data for his *Story of the Little Big Horn*, he won an interview with General Miles at his Washington home, and questioned him about the affidavit. All Miles would say was, "I believe Mrs. Custer has it." Colonel Graham then prevailed upon General Godfrey to approach Mrs. Custer on the matter. She found the document and turned it over to Godfrey. It had been sworn to by one Mary Adams, the devoted colored servant whom Mrs. Custer refers to in her books as Maria.

[28]Nelson A. Miles, *Serving the Republic* (New York, 1911), 189. After the Battle of Powder River, March 17, 1876, it was charged that Col. J. J. Reynolds, Third Cavalry, had abandoned a number of wounded soldiers to the Indians in his hasty withdrawal from the captured village.

The Great Debate

Generals Godfrey and W. S. Edgerly, and Col. Charles A. Varnum, all of whom had fought under Reno at the Little Bighorn, informed Colonel Graham that Mary Adams' testimony was worthless, for she had not even accompanied the 1876 expedition. Further substantiation turned up in testimony of Lt. C. L. Gurley, Sixth Infantry, who on July 6, 1876, went to the Custer home at Fort Lincoln to break the news of the Little Bighorn to Mrs. Custer. Gurley tells of waking Maria and sending her upstairs to summon Mrs. Custer. Colonel Graham also located the notary, George P. Flannery, before whom the affidavit was sworn. He was then living in St. Paul, Minnesota, but could not recall the details of the incident. In 1925, however, he told W. A. Falconer of Bismarck, North Dakota, that an Army officer had brought Mary Adams before him to execute the document. Although he could not remember with certainty, Flannery thought the officer was Lt. John Carland, Sixth Infantry, a notable Custer partisan. Miles had served in Dakota and Montana in 1878, the year the affidavit was sworn, and doubtless obtained it directly from Carland.[29]

During the 1920's the Army's Great Debate, now of 50 years standing, began to wear itself out as, one after another, the old soldiers who had fought at the Little Bighorn passed away. But the debate had already been taken up by the historian. A new school of writers appeared. Such men as Graham, Brininstool, Van de Water,

[29]These facts are drawn from a series of letters from Graham to the author, Dec. 1951 to Feb. 1952, but were later published in *The Custer Myth*, 279-82.

Dustin, DeLand, Hunt, Ghent, Kuhlman, and others made intensive studies of the evidence, and argued their conflicting interpretations even more vehemently than had the old soldiers. Now most of these men, too, have passed on. But others have taken their place, and the debate rages on.

While the partisans of the Great Debate were championing their particular favorites, another phase of Little Bighorn history was also unfolding. As the Army crushed the Sioux and herded them back to the reservation, the rush began for the Indian side of the story. Indian evidence offered unique problems of evaluation, even today dimly perceived by many historians, and injected fuel for more contention into the Custer Controversy. This evidence bore not so much on Custer's alleged disobedience of orders or Reno's alleged cowardice as on what actually happened on the Custer Battlefield. The mystery has yet to be solved to universal satisfaction and probably never will be; but the key to it undoubtedly lies in Indian testimony.

Curley, Crow Scout with Custer.

—*Haynes photo, from the Bowen Collection,*
Custer Battlefield Library.

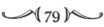

OUT OUR WAY

By J. R. Williams

The cartoonist get into the Custer controversy

Chapter IV

THE INDIAN SIDE OF THE STORY

LATE ON THE AFTERNOON of June 26, 1876, as Reno's exhausted men watched from the bluffs, the hostile exodus from the Little Bighorn Valley began. The Indians had discovered the approach of Terry and Gibbon, with infantry and cavalry bolstered by Gatling guns. Blanketing the prairie in a column three miles long and a half-mile wide, the tribes climbed the benchland west of the river and pointed toward the Bighorn Mountains.[1] Next day they turned back to the Little Bighorn, and in the following days traced their way down the Rosebud, across the Tongue, and into the valley of the Powder. Here, "sixteen sleeps" from the Little Bighorn, the unwieldy aggregation disbanded. The grass and game would no longer support so many.[2]

[1] Testimony of Lt. W. S. Edgerly in Graham, *Reno Court of Inquiry*, 399.
[2] Marquis, *A Warrior who Fought Custer*, 270-78.

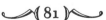

Terry and Gibbon did not pursue. They returned to the Yellowstone and paused to reorganize. Finally, early in August, they moved up the Rosebud and on the 10th met Crook marching down the stream. Both generals had been reinforced. They now went their separate ways, Terry ultimately to return to Fort Lincoln, Crook to aim for the Black Hills in a famous "starvation march."[3]

On the morning of September 9, 1876, Crook's advance guard, a battalion of the Third Cavalry under Capt. Anson Mills, stumbled on to the village of American Horse near Slim Buttes, on the northern tip of the Black Hills. Sending word of the discovery back to Crook, Mills charged the camp and scattered the inhabitants. American Horse was mortally wounded, but his men, reinforced by warriors from the nearby village of Crazy Horse, counterattacked and threw the cavalry on the defensive. Crook came to the rescue just in time to save the day. Amid the abandoned loot in the village, the troopers found a guidon lettered Troop I, Seventh Cavalry, and a pair of gauntlets stamped with Captain Keogh's name.

Farther north, Col. Nelson A. Miles and the Fifth Infantry built a cantonment at the mouth of Tongue River, and patrolled the line of the Yellowstone to head off flight of the Indians to the north. In mid-October he

[3]Principal sources for the Sioux wars, 1876-1881: Reports of the Secretary of War, 1876, 1877, 1880, 1881; Bourke, *On the Border with Crook;* Anson Mills, *My Story* (Washington, 1918); George B. Grinnell, *The Fighting Cheyennes* (New York, 1915); Hanson, *Conquest of the Missouri;* Miles, *Personal Recollections;* George E. Hyde, *Red Cloud's Folk: A History of the Oglala Sioux Indians* (Norman, 1937, 1957).

discovered almost 3,000 Sioux, including Sitting Bull and Gall. Two days of parleying with Sitting Bull demonstrated that he had no intention of surrendering unless the most extravagant terms were met. After two days of skirmishing, much the larger share of the Sioux, principally Miniconjou and Sans Arc, came in and surrendered.

Miles paroled them upon their promise to go to the Missouri River agencies, but held several chiefs as hostages. Sitting Bull and some 400 Hunkpapas scorned the path chosen by their kinsmen and made good their escape.

A month later Col. Ronald S. Mackenzie's Fourth Cavalry discovered Dull Knife's Cheyenne village wintering in a canyon on the north fork of Powder River. In a dawn attack, Mackenzie smashed into the village and drove the startled occupants into the bitter cold. They watched their winter stores go up in smoke as the soldiers destroyed the camp. Here also were reminders of the Custer Battle, including a roster book that once belonged to a sergeant of the Seventh Cavalry. The remnant of Dull Knife's people eventually made their way to Crazy Horse's camp on Box Elder Creek, where they were hospitably received by the Oglalas.

Throughout the long winter, one of the most severe on record, Miles allowed the hostiles no security in their winter camps. Their resolution wavered and finally collapsed. As winter gave way to spring, demoralized bands of Indians, numbering from 30 to 900, drifted southward into Nebraska and surrendered at Camps Sheridan and Robinson. During March 1877 over 2,200 Indians gave up. On April 22 Two Moon brought 303 destitute Cheyennes into Miles' cantonment on Tongue River. A number promptly donned the army blue, enlisting as scouts to aid in subduing their kinsmen who remained on the warpath.

Soon even Crazy Horse began to tire of the fugitive life. Spotted Tail, docile chief of the Brulé Sioux, who had remained at peace, was sent in April to negotiate with the great Oglala warrior. His efforts led at length to the surrender of Crazy Horse and Dull Knife with their combined following.

On May 7 Miles found Lame Deer's camp on the Rosebud. While infantrymen mounted on mules stampeded the pony herd, Miles sent a squadron of the Second Cavalry to storm the village. Lame Deer and Iron Star were killed, and their people scattered into the hills, then made their way to Nebraska and surrendered. By September the last of them had been received and resettled on the reservation.

This left only the intransigent Sitting Bull. Faced with disintegration of his victorious alliance, the Hunkpapa leader retreated northward and escaped across the international boundary. For the next two years the Hunkpapas lived in Canada, but followed the buffalo herds into Montana, where they committed depredations and kept the agency Indians constantly in a state of agitation.

In the spring of 1879 Miles advanced from his base, now named Fort Keogh, to clear northern Montana of these Indians. He skirmished with war parties along the border, and made it a dangerous undertaking for any of the fugitives to set foot on United States soil. The Queen could not feed the starving Sioux, and the buffalo grazed exasperatingly on the wrong side of a line ceaselessly patrolled by United States soldiers.

Unity of the Sioux leadership began to crack under the stress. First Gall, then Crow King slipped away with their bands and went to Fort Buford to surrender. Weakened by defections, Sitting Bull himself finally showed up at the fort on July 19, 1881. He had with him only 43 families, a mere shadow of the mighty coalition that had overwhelmed Custer.

During the spring and summer of 1881, the bulk of these Sioux were distributed among the agencies of the Great Sioux Reservation. Sitting Bull was placed aboard the steamer *Sherman* on July 29 and taken, after a pause at Standing Rock Agency, to Fort Randall for confinement as a prisoner of war. Two years later he was released and returned to Standing Rock to settle near the spot where he had been born.

✕   ✕   ✕

Why should the last fatal movements of Custer's men be shrouded in such mystery? The Indians were there. They saw what happened. Why could not they furnish the missing pieces of the puzzle? In fact, the rush to get the Indian side of the story began as soon as the vanguard of Custer's slayers drifted into the agencies in the autumn of 1876. Since then, the Sioux and Cheyennes have added scores of eye-witness accounts to the voluminous literature of the Little Bighorn. They have succeeded mainly in deepening the mystery and making it even more tantalizing than it was before the first Indian told his story.

Most of the Indian testimony is so confused, contradictory, and weirdly divorced from known reality that one is tempted to ignore all such evidence. This indeed was the decision of Col. W. A. Graham.

> As to the stories told by the Indians [he once wrote], there are so many of them, and so few that tie in with each other, that I found it impossible to reconcile them sufficiently to form a coherent narrative. I submitted the whole mess—upwards of 50 or 60 . . . to Gen. Hugh Scott . . . who knew more about Indians than any man of his generation . . . He agreed with me that the task was impossible, unless I summarily discredited some as false and accepted others as true . . . [This] I was unwilling to do.[4]

Others have been more reluctant to reject such potentially valuable material, but only a few, a very few indeed, have succeeded in doing more than make themselves look silly to all but the uninformed. The rest failed because they lacked insight into the character of Indian testimony and the manifold influences that produced distortion, incoherence, and falsehood.

This result sprang mainly from failure of white interrogator and red witness to achieve a meeting of the minds, especially when, as was usually the case, a third mind, that of an interpreter, intervened. Exact meaning is extremely difficult to convey from one language to another, and the average Sioux or Cheyenne interpreter

[4] W. A. Graham, in letter to *Westerners Brand Book* (Chicago), VII, 6 (August, 1950), 43.

was scarcely proficient in the science. Beyond this, many of the interrogators were newspaper reporters for whom historical accuracy was an objective distinctly secondary to sensational copy, and many of the witnesses had a variety of motives for not telling the truth.

Even the honest seeker of truth encountered enormous obstacles stemming from differences in cultural background. The existence of these he rarely even suspected. Testimony delivered from an aboriginal frame of reference but interpreted and recorded from a Caucasian frame of reference risked serious distortion in the process. Only the recorder who had actually lived among the Indians long enough to become familiar with their thought patterns could guard against construing their speech in terms of the background and experience of his own race.

Take for example the question of how Crazy Horse or Gall deployed their men against Custer's battalion, a question asked in one form or another by most interrogators. Such a query made little sense to the average Indian, for Indians did not fight in the same formal manner as the white man. War chiefs could not ordinarily make tactical dispositions because they possessed no command authority, as we understand the term. In combat, the warrior was an independent unit, and obeyed a particular chief only so long as it suited his fancy. The white man who asked how the Sioux chiefs marshaled their men assumed that Crazy Horse and Gall "commanded" the same as Custer and Reno. Moreover, in the cases of Gall and Two Moon, among others, he also assumed, because of their later notoriety on the reservation, an inflated conception of their rank at the time of the battle. If the response seems meaningless to the student, the question surely seemed meaningless to the Indian witness.

Besides their failure to recognize the influence of cultural differences, few interrogators could free themselves from the habit of asking leading questions drawn from preconceived but rarely correct theories. Confronted with a query that bore no relation to anything in his experience, the Indian answered with evasion, ambiguity, or sheer prevarication. Thus, imagine the quandary of the participant asked what the Sioux did when Custer tried to cross the river and charge the center of their village, when he may have come no closer to the river than one-half or three-quarters of a mile.

The character and disposition of the Indian himself offered even greater obstacles. When telling his story, the Indian emitted a disconcerting jumble of ephemeral, non-chronological impressions. He skipped indiscriminately from one incident to another without regard to time or place. To the white mind, the product was incoherence at its worst. There was the tendency to portray only what the individual narrator saw personally as applying to the battle as a whole. There was, finally, the inescapable truth that the American Indian was a showman and braggart. Boasting of great deeds in war was a time-honored custom that formed part of tribal ceremonies. Too often, as a result, the questioner was told what he wanted to hear, heavily laden with allusions to grandiose feats of heroism, instead of what actually happened.

Beyond all this, Indian participants had a very sound reason for not telling the whole truth, for now that the white man once more had them in his power, many undeniably feared reprisals. Discussing the story of Cheyenne participants that Custer's men committed mass suicide, Dr. Charles Kuhlman wrote that the Cheyennes

> may have adopted this fiction some time after the battle because many of them soon entered the service in the army as scouts or police where they learned that the white men felt pretty bad about the killing of "Long Hair" and his men. That made it a bit awkward and some kind of alibi seemed to be needed. It seems that not until after the semi-centennial exercises on the Custer field did the Cheyennes become fully convinced that the white man harbored no thoughts of reprisals. By that time the suicide story had been repeated so often that they seem to have forgotten that they had invented it. The Sioux do not mention wholesale suicides.[5]

Despite the complex of pitfalls that awaits the student of Indian evidence, it offers many clues to what happened in the Sioux and Cheyenne villages and on Custer Hill. The student, however, must be fully aware of the many sources of error; he must, to the highest degree possible, strive to think like an Indian when interpreting Indian evidence; he must study it against the background of intimate knowledge of the terrain; and he must

[5]Charles Kuhlman, "Tribune Writer Believed One of Last to Fall at Little Big Horn," *Bismarck* (No. Dak.) *Tribune,* (Golden Jubilee Edition), Aug. 15, 1939, p. 10.

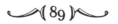

carefully compare it with all other evidence, both Indian and white. The Indian side of the story offers a challenging and potentially valuable source of knowledge, but it must be handled with extreme caution, and no one account may be considered, as it usually is, as the "true story of Custer's Last Stand" simply because the author was there.

✗   ✗   ✗

The first of the hostiles to give up in the fall of 1876 found interviewers waiting for them at the agencies. Thus a Hunkpapa named Kill Eagle contributed one of the earliest Indian versions of the Little Bighorn.[6] The western papers were still demanding a war of extermination, so Kill Eagle, while admitting his presence in the hostile camp on June 25, described himself as an unwilling observer who seized the first opportunity to steal away.

While the warriors were fighting Reno at the upper end of the village, said Kill Eagle, Custer was approaching the lower end, his presence concealed from the Indians by the bluffs east of the river. When he suddenly appeared, alarm and then panic swept the camp. The women began taking down the lodges and preparing for flight. But Reno's retreat released the fighting men on the south and they rushed through the village to meet the new threat from the north. Kill Eagle saw no more, for he was now heading in the opposite direction.

[6]*New York Herald,* Sept. 24, 1876; Oct. 6, 1876. Excerpts were later printed in Whittaker, *Life of Custer,* 592-93.

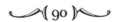

Indian Side of the Story

Of all the participants interviewed in the first year after the battle, Crazy Horse was the most prominent. He surrendered at Camp Robinson, Nebraska, in the spring of 1877, and shortly afterward Lt. William Philo Clark arranged for Charles Diehl, special correspondent for the *Chicago Times,* to talk with him. William Hunter interpreted, and Horned Horse acted as spokesman for Crazy Horse.[7]

Despite its brevity, the Crazy Horse narrative contains some important information concerning the makeup of the Indian alliance. Other participants later confirmed it. From south to north (upper to lower end), Crazy Horse described the arrangement of the village as follows: Hunkpapas under Sitting Bull, Oglalas under Crazy Horse, Miniconjous under Fast Bull, Sans Arc under Red Bear, Cheyennes under Ice Bear, Yanktonais and Santees under Inkpaduta (the same who figured in the Minnesota outbreak of 1862), and Blackfeet Sioux under Scabby Head. Black Moon, a Hunkpapa chief, was charged with general direction of the alliance, but he was killed early in the fighting. Crazy Horse estimated that the village contained 1,800 lodges and 400 wickiups (small, temporary brush shelters housing one or two occupants). This, the correspondent calculated, would total about 7,000 warriors. The arithmetic was Diehl's and its accuracy is questionable.

When asked about Indian casualties, Crazy Horse estimated that 58 were killed and 60 wounded. "From

[7]*Chicago Times,* May 27, 1877; Chicago *Inter-Ocean,* June 7, 1877; *Yankton Dakotaian,* June 7, 1877; "Crazy Horse's Story of the Custer Battle," South Dakota Historical Society, *Collections,* VI (Aberdeen, 1912), 224.

their way of expressing it," said Diehl, "I should judge that about 60 per cent of their wounded died."

Crazy Horse and Horned Horse asserted (and many Indians have since reiterated) that Reno's assault on the upper end of the village was a surprise, and created such consternation that the women flocked to the lower end. Had the Indians been expecting Custer, or as many would have it, had Custer ridden into a carefully prepared ambush, the women and children would long since have been moved to a place of negligible danger.

Unfortunately for history, Crazy Horse was marked for imprisonment at Dry Tortugas, Florida. The arrest was badly mismanaged and he was tricked into entering the guardhouse at Camp Robinson. When the duplicity of his captors became evident, he whipped out a knife and started hacking his way to freedom. A well-directed bayonet thrust ended the scuffle, and the mighty warrior of the Oglalas died in the night. The grieving Sioux buried his body at an unknown spot on the prairie.[8]

Horned Horse, who acted as Crazy Horse's spokesman in the audience with Diehl, gave his version of the Little Bighorn to Lieutenant Clark at Red Cloud Agency.[9] Horned Horse explained that he had lost a son at the beginning of the fight, and had gone to a hill overlook-

[8]See account and diary of Maj. Gen. Jesse M. Lee in E. A. Brininstool, *Crazy Horse* (Los Angles, 1949). Lee was a lieutenant in the Ninth Infantry in 1877, and was military agent in charge of Spotted Tail Agency. He was present when Crazy Horse was killed, but the Sioux leader told him shortly before dying that he held him in no way responsible for the stabbing. Lee will be remembered as Recorder at the Reno Court of Inquiry in 1879.

[9]Reproduced in John F. Finerty, *War-Path and Bivouac* (New York, 1890), 190-92. Finerty was the *Chicago Times'* correspondent with Crook in 1876.

ing the battlefield to mourn. From here, he said, he watched the spectacle. He offered the proposition that Custer rode down to the ford opposite the center of the village and tried to cross. Several men were devoured by quicksand, and the battalion withdrew to the ridges and fought bravely until all were killed. "The watercourse, in which most of the soldiers died, ran with blood. He had seen many massacres, but nothing to equal that."

The bit about the quicksand is a fantasy of the sort that often creeps into Indian accounts. As Clark was presumably an honest seeker of truth, and indeed quite adept in the sign language, it is unlikely that Horned Horse was misquoted. It made a good story and thrilled his white listeners, so he told it. This at least is a probable explanation. As a matter of fact, the ford contained no such quagmire as described. Benteen said at the Court of Inquiry that it was somewhat miry but presented no obstacle to crossing. Moreover, hundreds of warriors swarmed across the river here to meet Custer and drive him back to Custer Hill. It is now generally agreed by students of the battle that the battalion did not descend Medicine Tail Coulee to its mouth. Horned Horse doubtless had a sense of humor that escaped Lieutenant Clark, who should have been alerted when the stream began to run red with blood.

X   X   X

In 1877 Lt. Gen. Philip H. Sheridan decided to visit the Custer Battlefield as part of an inspection of frontier military installations. In preparation for the visit, his brother and military secretary, Col. Michael V. Sheridan, went in advance to tidy up the battlefield. Escorted by the Seventh Cavalry's rejuvenated Troop I, Capt. Henry J. Nowlan, Colonel Sheridan reached the site of the disaster on June 25, the first anniversary. The bodies of the slain were reburied where they had fallen and wooden stakes placed over each grave. The remains of Custer and most of the officers were taken up and shipped back East for reburial in cemeteries selected by next of kin. With impressive ceremonies, Custer himself was buried in the post cemetery at West Point Military Academy on October 10, 1877.[10]

Generals Sheridan, Crook, and their staffs, and Troop L, Fifth Cavalry, reached Custer Battlefield several weeks later. A dozen or so Brulés and Oglalas, veterans of the Little Bighorn, had been picked up at Red Cloud and Spotted Tail Agencies to show the Lieutenant General how it all happened. Reno's approach, these Indians explained, had not been detected until he was a mile or so above the village, and word of his presence was the first intimation the Indians had that soldiers were anywhere nearby. Consternation spread through the camp. Then Custer appeared across the river opposite the center of the village. Part of the warriors took on

---

[10]Hugh L. Scott, *Some Memories of a Soldier* (New York, 1928), 48, describes the visit of Colonel Sheridan's party. Scott, a lieutenant with Troop I, was present. He later became Chief of Staff of the Army. For an account of the Custer burial ceremony at West Point, see *Harper's Weekly*, Oct. 27, 1877.

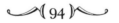

Reno, the rest Custer. They overcame the disadvantage of surprise and won the day.[11]

Later in the summer Lts. Philo Clark and J. W. Pope visited the battlefield in the company of two Sioux participants. The pair of Indians elaborated on Custer's descent of Medicine Tail Coulee toward the center of the camp. They said that, when Custer saw the tepees across the river, he dismounted and deployed, one troop some distance in advance of the others, at an angle to Custer Ridge. This troop, it was alleged, made a valiant fight and inflicted many casualties on the Indians.

Here is an example of the confusion of time and sequence often found in Indian accounts. As Custer rode down Medicine Tail Coulee toward the camp, the Gray Horse Troop is believed to have preceded the other four troops as described. But the same troop, some time later and a mile farther north, fought at an angle to Custer Ridge and inflicted severe casualties upon the Cheyennes in that quarter of the battlefield. The reader, however, is left with the impression that the incident took place on Medicine Tail Coulee at the beginning of the engagement.[12]

The following summer, 1878, Col. Nelson A. Miles arrived on the battleground with a group of Indians who

[11]The composite of the testimony given to the Sheridan party is in Homer Wheeler, *Buffalo Days* (Indianapolis, 1925), 154-80. Colonel Wheeler was a lieutenant with the Fifth Cavalry escort. See also Charles King, "Custer's Last Battle," *Harper's New Monthly Magazine*, LXXXI (August, 1890).

[12]E. S. Godfrey, "Custer's Last Battle," Montana Historical Society, *Contributions*, IX (Helena, 1923), 199. This is Godfrey's second article of the same title. It differs materially from the first, in *Century Magazine*, January 1892.

had fought there. He recorded the following opinions delivered by these participants:

> When asked what would have been the result if Reno had not retreated, the Indians frankly said that if he had not run, they would have fled. They were also asked what the consequences would have been if Reno with the seven troops had followed the Uncpapas and Ogalallas when they turned and went down to the assistance of the Indians in the village [threatened by Custer], and they candidly admitted that they would have been between two fires.[13]

✕ ✕ ✕

As an object of popular interest, no other Indian leader of the 19th century approached the stature of Sitting Bull. Known across the land as "the chief who wiped out Custer," he commanded the fascinated attention of the American people down to the day of his death. The two accounts of the Little Bighorn with which he endowed history gained a large audience in their day, but for obvious reasons have been all but forgotten by more recent students.

In 1877 Father J. B. M. Genin, a Catholic priest engaged in building a chain of missions along the Northern Pacific Railroad between Bismarck and Duluth, convinced himself that he could talk Sitting Bull into surrendering. He set out for the Hunkpapa stronghold in the Woody Mountains, in Canada, and there, during one

---

[13]Miles, *Personal Recollections,* 289.

of his many unsuccessful peace conferences, heard Sitting Bull tell how Custer had been annihilated.[14]

In this version, Sitting Bull's scouts maintained a close watch on Custer's movements. The women and children withdrew to safety in the hills as Custer came closer, and the village was prepared so that it looked like an ordinary, unsuspecting Sioux encampment. The warriors, however, lurked in the hills surrounding the empty camp. When Custer appeared, at the head of his regiment, several young warriors met him bearing a white flag. As Sitting Bull had prophesied, Custer murdered these emissaries of peace, then deployed his regiment and charged headlong into the dummy village. Before the troopers recovered from their surprise, the concealed warriors burst into their ranks from ambush and liquidated the entire regiment.

In 1879, Maj. L. E. F. Crozier of the Northwest Mounted Police visited Sitting Bull at Woody Mountain, and there learned the "true" story of Custer's Last Battle.[15]

Sitting Bull related how, in the weeks before the battle, he and Custer exchanged messages. Custer arrogantly demanded that the Sioux fight him. Sitting Bull refused.

[14]Linda W. Slaughter, "Leaves from Northwestern History," North Dakota Historical Society, *Collections*, I (Bismarck, 1902), 273-79. Miss Slaughter was a pioneer resident of Bismarck and correspondent of Father Genin, in one of whose letters this narrative was contained.

[15]W. N. Sage, "Sitting Bull's Own Narrative of the Custer Fight,"*Canadian Historical Review*, XVI (June, 1935), 171-75. Judson Elliott Walker, *Campaigns of General Custer in the Northwest and the Final Surrender of Sitting Bull* (1881), 86-103, recounts the substance of the Sitting Bull stories, as well as the narratives of some of the other recently surrendered hostiles.

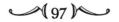

He wished only to be left alone to live in peace. Finally, he saw that Custer was not a man of reason and prepared his men for action. Waving a flag aloft, and exhorting his warriors to show courage, he reduced Reno's hapless command to a fragment of five soldiers and an interpreter. The interpreter shouted that Custer was with the other detachment and, since the fight was a personal one, Sitting Bull spared these fortunates and turned his wrath on Custer at the other end of the village.

At the moment the Sioux hordes clashed with Custer's battalion, a great thunder storm enveloped the battlefield, and many soldiers were struck down by lightning. This divine intervention demonstrated conclusively that the Great Spirit favored the Sioux. Custer's force was destroyed and, again sparing five soldiers and an interpreter, the Chief withdrew his army.

Sitting Bull's actual role in the fight is not easily assessed. His biographer, Stanley Vestal, contended that he was in the thick of the battle against Major Reno and was conspicuous for his leadership and courage, but that he did not reach the Custer Battlefield until after the fighting had ended. Others have said that, as a medicine man, he took no part in the battle. General Sheridan's Sioux guides in 1877 pointed out the spot on the benchlands west of the valley where Sitting Bull made the medicine that won the day for the Indians. And James McLaughlin, the Hunkpapa agent during the 1880's, declared that all the Sioux he had quizzed stated that, upon the approach of the cavalry, Sitting Bull withdrew to the hills to make medicine. Whatever the truth, there is little doubt that his leadership was the decisive factor in putting together and holding together the coalition of tribes that proved Custer's undoing.[16]

For a time during the middle eighties, Sitting Bull toured the country as an attraction of Buffalo Bill's Wild West. With this one exception, however, he remained haughty and aloof from the white man to the tragic end of his life. He became a leader in the Messiah religion that swept the plains tribes in 1890. Fearing his influence, Gen. Nelson A. Miles ordered his arrest. On December 15, 1890, Indian policemen entered his cabin on Grand River to take him into custody. Fighting broke out, and he was killed by a member of his own race, Sergeant Red Tomahawk. The Ghost Dance War that followed, culminating in the Battle of Wounded Knee Creek on December 29, was the last stand of the Sioux Nation. Ironically, the trumpets of the Seventh Cavalry sounded this final note in the pageant of the Indian wars.

⚔ ⚔ ⚔

In the fall of 1881, the surrender of Sitting Bull aroused fresh interest in the Custer Battle, and reporters set forth to record the stories of the Indians who had fled to Canada four years earlier. At Fort Yates, adjacent to Standing Rock Agency, Low Dog and Crow King were persuaded to talk about the Little Bighorn. Low Dog proved quite voluble, and in fact grew so eloquent that he attracted an intent audience, among which were sev-

[16]Stanley Vestal, *Sitting Bull, Champion of the Sioux* (Boston, 1932; Norman, 1957), Ch. 23; Wheeler, *Buffalo Days,* 182; James McLaughlin, *My Friend the Indian* (Boston, 1910), 165 *passim.*

eral officers of the Seventh Cavalry who had fought on Reno Hill.[17]

Low Dog injected another element of controversy to confound the white man's attempt at reconstructing the disaster. He said that Custer's men all dismounted, and tried to fight on foot and hold their mounts at the same time. The frightened horses became unmanageable, plunged and dragged their masters, deflected their fire, and generally lowered combat effectiveness. Did Custer permit his men to fight other than in the classic cavalry fashion, wherein every fourth man leads four horses to the rear, freeing the other three to fight on foot? Or was the Sioux onslaught so sudden and overwhelming that he had no control over his men? Or did Low Dog refer only to horseholders and led horses when he pictured rearing, kicking horses dragging their attendants to and fro and stampeding with saddle bags full of precious ammunition?

Low Dog described Indian tactics at the Little Bighorn as a charge *en masse* on Custer's dismounted command, another point of some dispute among authorities. "I called to my men," said Low Dog, "'This is a good day to die; follow me.' We massed our men, and that no man should fall back, every man whipped another man's horse, and we rushed right on them." Later, Crow King, Iron Thunder, and Hump agreed that this was the way the Sioux crushed Custer.[18] Still others disagreed. The

---

[17]"Low Dog's Story of the Custer Fight," *Army and Navy Journal*, Aug. 13, 1881. The account first appeared in the *Cincinnati Commercial*.

[18]*Leavenworth Weekly Times*, Aug. 18, 1881, typed copy furnished by Col. W. A. Graham.

Tenth Anniversary Group at Fort Custer, June 25, 1886. Survivors of the Little Bighorn are designated thus: (1) Captain Thomas M. McDougall, 7th Cavalry; (2) Major Frederick W. Benteen, 9th Cavalry; (3) Colonel Nathan A. M. Dudley, 1st Cavalry; (4) Second Lieutenant Edwin P. Brewer, 7th Cavalry; (5) Dr. Henry R. Porter; (6) Second Lieut. James D. Mann, 7th Cavalry; (7) Mr. Tingle, St. Paul Globe; (8) Captain Frank D. Garretty, 17th Infantry; (10) Captain Edward S. Godfrey, 7th Cavalry; (11) Fred Benteen; (12) First Lieutenant Herbert E. Slocum, 7th Cavalry; (13) Second Lieutenant Joseph McD. T. Partello, of the 5th Infantry.

—David F. Barry photo, from the Bowen Collection,
Custer Battlefield Library.

Tenth Anniversary Group on Custer Hill, June 25, 1886. (1) Corporal Hall; (2) Sergeant Horn; (3) Captain T. M. McDougall; (4) Mrs. J. D. Mann; (5) Major F. W. Benteen; (6) Captain E. S. Godfrey; (7) Mrs. F. W. Benteen; (8) Dr H. R. Porter; (9) Mrs. F. D. Garretty; (10) Captain W. S. Edgerly; (11) Trumpeter Penwell; (12) White Swan, Crow Scout

—*David F. Barry photo, from the Bowen Collection, Custer Battlefield Library.*

warriors, they said, dismounted and crept forward toward Custer in the high grass. Without exposing themselves to the fire of the soldiers, they shot clouds of arrows into the air to converge on the knot of defenders on Custer Hill. Which method was used no one knows to this day—possibly a combination of both.

Low Dog agreed with the Sioux who went to the field with Colonel Miles in 1878: "If Reno and his warriors had fought as Custer and his warriors fought," he said, "the battle might have gone against us. No white man fought as bravely as Custer and his men."

Concluding, the Sioux leader estimated Indian casualties at 38 killed and a great many—"I can't tell the number"—wounded who died later.

Crow King confined himself to a few general remarks underlining some points brought out by Low Dog. Had Reno held out in the valley and fought as Custer fought, he believed, the Indians would have been forced to divide in order to protect their women and children. He expressed admiration for Custer, and said that the fight had so impressed the Indians with military prowess that they realized the futility of prolonged hostility.

In interpreting and evaluating these narratives, it is well to note the context in which they were given. Two warriors just off the warpath, uncertain of their future, were recounting to a group that included members of the Seventh Cavalry the story of how they butchered portions of the Seventh Cavalry. As Dr. Kuhlman remarked, the Indians learned that the white men felt pretty badly about the death of Custer.

Custer and the Great Controversy

One of the most widely publicized Indian accounts was that of the Sioux chief Red Horse. His story, illustrated by a surprisingly accurate map and pictographic characters, was recorded in 1881 by Dr. Charles E. Mc-Chesney, Army surgeon who later served as agent for the Miniconjous of Cheyenne River Agency.[19]

Red Horse was in his lodge at the center of the village when four women called his attention to a cloud of dust rising over the valley above the camp. The cloud soon yielded soldiers, causing pandemonium among the Indians. Red Horse rushed to the council lodge, where presumably the chiefs would deliberate the next move! But the chiefs had no time for discussion, for "the soldiers came so quickly that we could not talk. We came out of the council lodge and talked in all directions. The Sioux mount horses, take guns, and go fight soldiers. Women and children mount horses, and go, meaning get out of the way."

After the Sioux had driven Reno back to the bluffs and surrounded him, "A Sioux came and said that a different party of soldiers had all the women and children prisoners. Like a whirlwind the word went around, and the Sioux . . . left the soldiers on the hill and went quickly to save the women and children." They met Custer's battalion and pushed it back to the ridge. There "these soldiers," declared Red Horse, slipping into the irrationality

[19]Garrick Mallery, "Picture Writing of the American Indians," *Tenth Annual Report of the Bureau of American Ethnology*, 1888-89 (Washington, 1893), 563-66. Reproduced in J. L. Humfreville, *Twenty Years Among Our Hostile Indians* (Hartford, 1899), 357-77; *Teepee Book*, June 1916 and 1926; and *Cavalry Journal*, July 1, 1926.

that came so easily to Indians extolling their triumphs, "became foolish, many throwing away their guns and raising their heads saying, 'Sioux, pity us; take us prisoners.'"

Red Horse's principal contribution turned on his alusion to the "bravest man the Sioux ever fought." Such a distinction was not conferred lightly by the Sioux, and the identity of the "bravest man" became a matter for intriguing speculation. Red Horse described him thus:

> Among the soldiers was an officer who rode a horse with four white feet. The Sioux had for a long time fought many brave men of different people, but the Sioux say this officer was the bravest man they ever fought . . . This officer wore a large brimmed hat and a deerskin coat. This officer saved the lives of many soldiers by turning his horse and covering the retreat. Sioux say this officer is the bravest man they ever fought.

Unhappily, Red Horse failed to specify whether this feat occurred during Reno's flight from the valley or Custer's defense of the ridge to the north. Dr. Charles Kuhlman contended that the officer was Capt. Myles W. Keogh, commander of Troop I in Custer's battalion. By extraordinary and complicated reasoning, he deduced that only Keogh had the opportunity to shield his men in the manner portrayed by Red Horse.[20] Kuhlman discounted Red Horse's assertion that the officer's mount had four white feet. Comanche, Keogh's illustrious mount, was a claybank dun, with no trace of white on

[20]Luce, *Keogh, Comanche and Custer*, 59 ff.; and Kuhlman, *Legend into History*, 206-207, 67, note.

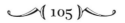

his feet. Custer, likewise attired in buckskin, rode a horse, Vic, with three white feet. But according to Kuhlman's construction, Custer had shot his horse for a breastwork with the group on Custer Hill.

Some students believe that Red Horse referred to M Troop's Capt. Thomas H. French, also buckskin-clad, in Reno's retreat from the valley to the bluffs. French himself thought Red Horse referred to him. In a letter to a Chicago acquaintance in 1880, he roundly condemned Reno's precipitate flight from the timber (the *sauve qui peut* movement, he called it on another occasion), and related how he constituted himself a one-man rear guard unit to parry the bold thrusts of the Sioux at the fleeing troops. Confronted with this letter, Kuhlman countered with testimony to show that French, far from being in the rear, was among the first to reach the river.[21]

And so the identity of the "bravest man the Sioux ever fought" remains a mystery.

✗ ✗ ✗

As the tenth anniversary of the Custer Fight drew near, some of the surviving officers arranged to gather on the battlefield for a reunion. The country had changed in a decade. Completion of the Northern Pacific Railroad had opened Montana to settlement. A military post, Fort Custer, now guarded the junction of the Bighorn and

[21] French's letter is quoted in unpublished manuscript critique by Col. W. A. Graham of Kuhlman's *Legend Into History* manuscript, furnished by Colonel Graham. Kuhlman's evidence regarding French is in Kuhlman's reply, also furnished by Graham. French's *sauve qui peut* quip is in unpublished narrative of the Custer Battle by W. S. Edgerly in the E. B. Custer Collection, Custer Battlefield National Monument, Mont.

Indian Side of the Story

Little Bighorn Rivers, and the Custer Battlefield, 15 miles up the Little Bighorn, had become a major tourist attraction. A monument bearing the names of the dead dominated the countryside from the crest of Custer Hill. Cut of Vermont granite, it had been shipped to Fort Custer in three sections and erected during the spring of 1881 by Lt. C. F. Roe and Troop M, Second Cavalry. Shortly afterward the bodies of the soldiers had been reinterred in a mass grave dug around the base of the shaft.[22]

Besides a large delegation of officers and ladies from Forts Custer and Keogh, those who attended the anniversary celebration included Major Benteen, Captains Godfrey (who organized the pilgrimage), Edgerly, and McDougall; and Dr. Porter. Through the influence of Agent James McLaughlin of the Standing Rock Agency, the Hunkpapa Chief Gall had been persuaded to accompany the officers and relate his version of the battle.[23] Gall's account, delivered on the field, was distinguished by absence of boastfulness and a diplomatic regard for the feelings of his listeners, whose comrades his warriors had slain.

Gall emphasized, contrary to contemporary opinion, that Custer did not reach the ford opposite the center of

[22]Report of the Secretary of War, 1881, I, 92, 97-98.

[23]Descriptions of the anniversary gathering are in *Army and Navy Journal*, July 3, 1886; Godfrey, "Custer's Last Battle," Montana Historical Society, *Contributions*, *op. cit.*; Lt. Col. W. H. C. Bowen in C. T. Brady, *Northwestern Fights and Fighters* (New York, 1907). Gall's story, as given to the reunion party, has been published in *Army and Navy Journal*, July 3, 1886; Edward Ellis, *Indian Wars of the United States* (New York, 1892); Frances Holley, *Once Their Home* (Chicago, 1890); and Finerty, *War-Path and Bivouac*.

the Indian camp. He was heading for the ford when Gall's warriors intercepted him about a mile up the bed of Medicine Tail Coulee and drove him north against Custer Ridge. There,

> The soldiers got their shells stuck in their guns and had to throw them away [The Springfield carbine had a faulty extractor]. Then they fought with their little guns [pistols]. The Indians were in couples behind and in front of Custer as he moved up the ridge, and there were as many as the grass on the plains. The first two companies [I and L, Keogh and Calhoun] dismounted and fought on foot. They never broke but retired step by step until forced back to the ridge on which all finally died. They were shot down in line where they stood.

The horseholders herded the soldiers' mounts, bearing pouches of reserve ammunition, to the rear. "The warriors directed a special fire against the troops who held the horses," he said, "and as soon as the holder was hit, by waving blankets and great shouting the horses were stampeded, which made it impossible for the soldiers to escape." In less than an hour they had all fallen. The Indians rode jubilantly over the field, shooting up the bodies. They were thus engaged when Captain Weir's troops, hastening without Reno's authority to the sound of the firing, appeared on the high hill four miles to the south. Weir could not, therefore, according to Gall, have altered the fate of Custer.

During the anniversary proceedings, Godfrey recalled many years later, he and several others were sitting in front of the monument questioning Gall when everyone, including the Sioux Chief, grew suspicious of the interpreter. His volubility suggested that he might be padding the translation. Gall abruptly rose, glanced meaningfully at Godfrey, and rode out along the ridge. Godfrey followed. On the L Troop positions at the southeast end of the battle ridge, Gall enacted for Godfrey a pantomime of the action on that part of the field. He

> silently surveyed the surroundings a few minutes [wrote Godfrey in 1923], when he pointed out the direction of the approach, indicating, now rapid and now slow march, according to the ground; then the halt, the dismounting of a part and the forward movement of the other troops deploying as skirmishers, opening out his fingers to show this movement, the other troops following, then these latter made a rapid move to the right front towards Custer Hill. Turning to me he told me to dismount; then he said, "You soldier, me Sioux," and put me in several positions of the troops, indicating them; during this he indicated the lines of approach of his own warriors, the stampede of the led horses, the driving back of the soldiers, the final stand. Then the disposition of his warriors; some dismounted near the crest, rising and dropping to draw the fire to cause waste of ammunition; the mounted warriors were lower down on the hillside. Then he imitated the war whoop in a low tone, the quirting of the ponies and the final charge.

Gall's account is one of the most coherent on record, probably because the recorder, Godfrey, was himself an intelligent interrogator close to the events described. It may be, however, that the narrative in places contains a bit more of Godfrey than of Gall, for it neatly supports Godfrey's own theories. Whether Godfrey shaped Gall's statements to fit his own hypotheses, or Gall's story shaped Godfrey's hypotheses as later published, is a matter of speculation. As already stated, the process of translating Indian accounts involves abstractions that are difficult to cope with.

Gall was an Indian of exceptional intelligence and character. When he surrendered, he renounced the warpath forever and worked closely with Agent McLaughlin, often in the face of hostility from his own people, to soften the impact of the white man's civilization. He sought constantly to impress upon his people the necessity of conforming to the new and alien way of life thrust upon them. With John Grass, he became a judge of Standing Rock's Indian court. During the Messiah craze of 1890, he counselled moderation in opposition to the extremism of Sitting Bull. Gall died at his home at Standing Rock in 1896.[24]

Gall's agent, James McLaughlin, made his contribution to the Indian side of the story, too. He obtained the narrative of Mrs. Spotted Horn Bull, an accomplished Sioux woman who vividly described the movements of the warriors and the scene in the village on the day of the battle. Her verbatim account, together with McLaughlin's observations as gleaned from a long and fruitful association with the Hunkpapas, was published as part of McLaughlin's autobiography in 1910.

✗   ✗   ✗

[24]DeLorme Robinson, "Pizi (Gall)," South Dakota Historical Society, *Collections*, I (1902), 152-53.

Indian Side of the Story

Cheyenne contributions found their way into print comparatively late, probably because the Cheyenne reservation on Montana's Tongue River was more remote than the Missouri River agencies of the Sioux. In 1898, however, writer Hamlin Garland journeyed to the Northern Cheyenne agency at Lame Deer to secure the story of Two Moon, prominent leader in the Cheyenne camp at the lower end of the hostile village on the Little Bighorn.[25]

Two Moon told Garland that after Reno's repulse he rode through the village to the Cheyenne camp and stopped the women from their panicky efforts to take down and flee with the lodges. "While I was sitting on my horse I saw flags coming up over the hill to the east. . . . Then the soldiers rose all at once . . . They formed in three bunches . . . Then a bugle sounded, and they all got off their horses, and some soldiers led the horses back over the hill."

Two Moon then described how the Sioux enveloped Custer from all sides, the Cheyennes going "up the left way," meaning they took part in the flanking movement under Crazy Horse that struck Custer unexpectedly at the north end of the battle ridge. "The smoke was like a great cloud, and everywhere the Sioux went the dust rose like smoke. We circled all around him—swirling like water round a stone. We shoot, we ride fast, we shoot again. Soldiers drop, and horses fall on them."

[25]Hamlin Garland, "General Custer's Last Fight as Seen by Two Moon," *McClure's Magazine.* XI (September, 1898), 446-48.

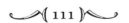

After most of the men on Custer Hill had fallen, a group of men—"may be so forty"—broke for the river. A man on a sorrel horse with a white face and forelegs, wearing a buckskin jacket, was in the van. (He was the "bravest man," according to Two Moon.) They were slaughtered as they ran, but one man succeeded in outdistancing his pursuers. "I thought he was going to escape, but a Sioux fired and hit him in the head. He wore braids on his arms [a sergeant]." Today, white marble headstones, 48 in number, are scattered from Custer Hill over the flat and into a deep ravine southwest of the monument, toward the river. On a ridge north of Medicine Tail Coulee, over a half-mile from any known comrade, the body of 1st Sgt. James Butler was found, and is now marked by a marble headstone.

Two Moon gave Indian losses as 39 Sioux and 7 Cheyennes killed, and about 100 wounded.

The Cheyennes found their most eloquent spokesmen in George Bird Grinnell and Dr. Thomas B. Marquis. Grinnell, a distinguished editor, author, naturalist and explorer, had accompanied Custer into the Black Hills in 1874. He spent much time among the Cheyennes, learned their customs and thought patterns, and won a degree of affection and confidence not often accorded a white man by Indians. He patiently and diplomatically drew from them their story of the Little Bighorn, which was published in *The Fighting Cheyennes* in 1915. A two-volume work, *The Cheyenne Indians*, followed in 1923.

Indian Side of the Story

Doctor Marquis was for many years reservation physician at the Lame Deer Agency. He achieved a place in Cheyenne affections second only to Grinnell. His story of Wooden Leg, *A Warrior Who Fought Custer*, was published in 1931, and is a model of Indian history. In addition, Marquis authored a series of pamphlets dealing with specialized aspects of Cheyenne history concerning the Little Bighorn.

X   X   X

Of all interpreters of Indian history, one of the most prolific in the 20th century was Stanley Vestal. He spent much time and effort interviewing old Sioux in the Dakotas, and in the 1930's produced several books based on the mass of material he had so painstakingly accumulated.[26] Great writer that he was, however, Vestal never escaped the trap that snares so many students of Indian history—the tendency to accept Indian evidence uncritically. Vestal's works represent in truth a substantial contribution to the history of the Little Bighorn and of the Sioux, but because of his historical method they must be used with the same caution one should apply to any other Indian evidence.

Not so the works of Vestal's contemporary, George Hyde. Once an assistant to George Bird Grinnell, Hyde apparently profited in this respect from the experience of Grinnell. His histories of the Sioux[27] exhibit a healthy

[26]*Sitting Bull, Champion of the Sioux* (Boston, 1932; Norman, 1956); *Warpath* (Boston, 1933); *New Sources of Indian History* (Norman, 1934).

[27]*Red Cloud's Folk: A History of the Oglala Sioux Indians* (Norman, 1937, 1957); *Spotted Tail's Folk: A History of the Brulé Sioux* (Norman, 1961).

skepticism, an awareness of the unique character of Indian evidence, and a constant checking of Indian evidence against other evidence. Had Vestal applied the techniques of Hyde, together they would have produced a remarkably complete history of the Sioux.

✗ ✗ ✗

Thus it is apparent from this tiny sampling of Indian testimony that the only witnesses to the annihilation of Custer utterly failed to clear up the mystery of how it happened. But it is apparent, too, that there are significant areas of agreement between Indian accounts, and that the mystery is not, in some respects, quite so bewildering as it was before they were recorded. One cannot emerge from a study of Indian testimony without the thought that it may some day, if sifted through the right mental equipment, unravel the enigma of the Little Bighorn.

"He stood like a sheaf of corn with all the ears fallen around him."
Errol Flynn as General Custer, at the last stand.

—*Courtesy Warner Brothers Pictures, Inc.*

Errol Flynn, as Custer, makes his last stand beside 7th Cavalry banner

—*Courtesy Warner Brothers Pictures, Inc*

Chapter V

THE LEGEND OF THE LITTLE BIGHORN

MORE THAN 85 YEARS have passed since George Armstrong Custer led the Seventh Cavalry into the Little Bighorn Valley and immortality. But today Custer's Last Stand still grips both amateur and professional historians with fascination. Over 150,000 visitors annually follow the road to the crest of the bleak Montana ridge where Custer died. Myriad publications each year revive the burning controversies and emphasize the oft-repeated myths. Radio, motion pictures, and television bring the heroics of the Little Bighorn to young and old alike. Since the June day in 1876 when Sioux bullets ended his brief but spectacular career, the legend of George Armstrong Custer has grown to extraordinary proportions. And year after year it continues to grow.

X   X   X

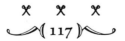

In actual fact, Custer's career was incredible enough. In the short span of 20 years he had hit top and bottom time and again. Despite a singularly unpromising record at West Point, he rose to the rank of major general at the age of 25. He rode to Appomattox at the head of a division of Sheridan's cavalry, yet the close of the war found him still a captain in the regular army. He was court-martialed and suspended from the Army, yet within a year he led his regiment in a smashing victory over Black Kettle's Cheyennes on the Washita. He explored the Black Hills and found gold there, yet within two years he met his death in a battle that was one of the most crushing defeats ever sustained by American troops.

In legend, however, even this record has been magnified and distorted beyond recognition. Every phase of Custer's career, and even the facts of his ancestry, are subjects of a mass of contradictory myths and biased interpretations. Such distortion can be partly explained by the emotional extremes Custer's personality inspired in his contemporaries. They either loved or hated him, and the views many of them set to paper reflected this conflict. For this reason alone, he would have been assured a controversial role in history. But it was the last stand at the Little Bighorn that focused widespread attention on his entire career and embedded the Custer legend forever in the folklore of America.

The Battle of the Little Bighorn not only climaxed a dramatic life, but immediately became a subject of fascination, controversy, and speculation. The disaster to

Custer's command, like the overwhelming of the Texans at the Alamo, left no survivor to tell what happened. The rescue column found the unclad, unmutilated body of Custer, pierced by two bullets, lying amid the scattered bodies of his men and the carcasses of their horses. The details of the fighting could only be guessed at. But the American people demanded to know both what had happened and how it had happened. Correspondents on the frontier obliged by filling the gaps in the story with material derived largely from fertile imaginations. Other writers not only copied the newspaper accounts but added their own embellishments. The result was a collection of myths that came to be accepted as the true story of the Custer Battle.

During the next 85 years, scores of novels and many self-proclaimed authentic histories repeated the well-worn tales of the early writers. Today, Errol Flynn stands "like a sheaf of corn with all ears fallen around him," waiting for the Sioux lance that will end his life and a three-hour motion picture. Children sit in rapt wonder before the television set, watching hordes of Sioux warriors swarm over the little band of cavalrymen and deal the mortal blow to "Yellow Hair." And after 85 years, the "only survivors" of a battle from which no man escaped number far more than the 230 men who died there.

✗   ✗   ✗

We saw in Chapter II how the newspapers laid the foundation for the Custer Controversy. They also laid the foundation for the growth of legend and myth. Accounts of the battle, largely or wholly fictional, were printed in a style that both expressed and appealed to the emotional Victorian temperament. One example will suffice.

> In that mad .charge up the narrow ravine, with the rocks above raining down lead upon the fated three hundred, with fire spouting from every bush ahead, with the wild, swarming horsemen circling along the heights like shrieking vultures waiting for the moment to sweep down and finish the bloody tale, every form, from private to general, rises to heroic size, and the scene fixes itself indelibly upon the mind. "The Seventh fought like tigers," says the dispatch; yea, they died as grandly as Homer's demigods. In the supreme moment of carnage, as death's relentless sweep gathered in the entire command, all distinctions of name and rank were blended, but the family that "died at the head of their column" will lead the throng when history recalls their deed . . . Success was beyond their grasp, so they died—to a man.[1]

The *New York Herald* began a subscription campaign to collect money enough for a monument to General Custer. Its pages for many weeks were crowded with letters to the editor. One, signed "School Girl," reveals the impact of the newspaper stories:

> I enclose ten cents (all I can spare), for a monument to the noble General Custer. I am a schoolgirl, but can read the newspapers, and my heart was filled with pity when I read the other night for mother the account in your paper of the awful slaughter done by the Indians on General

[1]*New York Herald*, July 13, 1876.

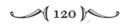

Custer and his army. We girls admire brave men, because, I suppose, and as mother says, we are such cowards ourselves. I would have given the world to have had one look at the fearless General Custer; and then he was so young and, as the papers say, so handsome. I could cry tears over his sad fate. All the girls and women, I fancy, must feel as I do, for such heroes as General Custer are what they most admire, and then, you know, they are scarce. Leave it to the schoolgirls and a monument will soon be raised to the gallant General Custer, for he was a man.[2]

X   X   X

The popular writers took up where the correspondents and editorial writers left off. Frederick Whittaker's *Life of Custer* set the tone. In it, Custer was a model of "Truth and sincerity, honor and bravery, tenderness, sympathy, unassuming piety and temperance," and "As a soldier there is no spot on his armor."[3] Whittaker's portrayal of Custer and his version of the Battle of the Little Bighorn mightily influenced his successors. To examine the popular Custer literature of the 1880's and 1890's is to read Whittaker again and again. One author after another drew his information directly and solely from Whittaker. And many actually copied, without credit, whole passages of the *Life of Custer*. In this manner the stories invented by the press and repeated by Whittaker gained extremely wide circulation. What they lacked in accuracy, they made up in repetition.

X   X   X

[2]*Ibid.*
[3]Whittaker, *Life of Custer*, 628.

⌐⟨ 121 ⟩⌐

Parenthetically, another influence that intensified the Custer legend should be noted. The General's devoted widow worked tirelessly the rest of her life to defend and elevate the name of her husband. She collaborated closely with Frederick Whittaker, and strongly conditioned the image of Custer that emerged from Whittaker's *Life*. She also wrote three books of her own—*Boots and Saddles* (1885), *Following the Guidon* (1890), and *Tenting on the Plains* (1893)—all of which ranked among the best sellers of the day. Making almost no effort to discuss her husband's professional life, by figuratively taking her readers into their homes at remote frontier forts and intimately portraying an idyllic life with a saintly mate, she worked herself and the memory of "Her General" into the hearts of the nation.

There were few, even among Custer's enemies, who did not admire the personable little lady. And many who might have been his bitterest critics withheld their fire out of consideration for Libby's feelings. There is little question that there existed, as Fred Dustin put it, a "conspiracy of silence" among those who disliked Custer. They seem to have tacitly agreed to wait until she had passed on to attack the General publicly. But she outlived them all, surviving her husband through 57 years of adoring memory, and died at the venerable age of 93 in April 1933.

It was impossible not to like Elizabeth Custer, either in person or through her writings, and it is not surprising that many who had no other standard of comparison came to see the General through her eyes. The picture of him that takes shape in her writings is of a giant among men. Such a man was perfectly capable of being and doing all the pulp writers said.

✗ ✗ ✗

It would be a Herculean chore to catalog and dissect even a small fraction of the most popular myths that have sprung from the early newspaper and pulp writers. Two will serve to illustrate the character of all.

Of all the myths of Custer and the Little Bighorn, the greatest variety and originality are to be found in the attempts to describe the details of Custer's death. Journalists, novelists, historians, and script-writers have killed Custer time and again and by every conceivable means.

Frederick Whittaker got them off to a rousing start. In the *Life of Custer*, he related how Curley, the friendly Crow Indian scout whom the newspapers built into an "only survivor," saw that Custer's command was hopelessly surrounded and faced with certain destruction. He went to his commander and offered to show him how to escape. But Custer "dropped his head to his breast and thought a moment," then "looked at Curley, waved him away and rode back to his little group of men, to die with them." And magnificently he did die. When "only a few officers were left alive, the Indians made a hand to hand charge, in which Custer fought like a tiger with his saber when his last shot was gone." He "killed or wounded three Indians with his saber" before receiving his mortal wound.[4]

[4]*Ibid.,* 599, 601.

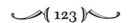

Custer and the Great Controversy

A typical sample of the many bizarre reconstructions that followed, and one that drew its inspiration chiefly from Whittaker, appeared in J. W. Buel's *Heroes of the Plains*, published five years after the battle. In the absence of any witness to provide the details set forth, Buel's omniscience was indeed as formidable as his prose.

> . . . men had sunk down beside their gallant leader until there was but a handful left, only a dozen, bleeding from many wounds, and hot carbines in their stiffening hands. The day is almost done, when, look! heaven now defend him, the charm of his life is broken, for Custer has fallen; a bullet cleaves a pathway through his side, and as he falters another strikes his noble breast. Like a strong oak stricken by the lightning's bolt, shivering the mighty trunk and bending the writhing branches down close to the earth, so fell Custer; but like the reacting branches, he rises partly up again and striking out like a fatally wounded giant lays three more Indians dead and breaks his mighty sword on the musket of the fourth; then, with useless blade and empty pistol falls back the victim of a dozen wounds. He is the last to succumb to death, and dies, too, with the glory of accomplished duty in his conscience and the benediction of a grateful country on his head.[5]

For all anyone knows, Custer may have fallen at any stage of the fighting. Even the Indians who killed him, if the best Indian testimony can be credited, did not know they were fighting Custer's cavalry, much less recognize the commander personally. Morever, with a little extra research, Buel might have ascertained that none of the cavalrymen, not even the officers, carried

[5]J. W. Buel, *Heroes of the Plains* (St. Louis, 1881), 391.

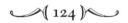

sabers, and that Custer died of two bullet wounds, not a dozen.

Contrasting sharply with the heroics portrayed by Buel was the theory of a group of writers who believed that Custer had committed suicide. The leading exponent of this thesis was Col. Richard I. Dodge, aide-de-camp to General Sherman. In 1882, Colonel Dodge published *Our Wild Indians*, a work that embodied his observations of the plains Indian during a long career in the West. Dodge pointed out that Custer's body was neither scalped nor mutilated, good evidence that he was a suicide. The Indian mutilated his victims, explained Dodge, because he believed it caused torment to their souls. Suicide, however, was an act evoking religious awe, and was so rare among Indians that it constituted big medicine. "Whatever the special religious opinion of each Indian in regard to taking the scalp of slain enemies," concluded Dodge, "I have never yet known a single case where the scalp of a suicide was stripped off."[6]

On the other hand, many scholars who have studied the unique Custer personality agree that, whatever may have been Custer's other faults, he never lacked courage. Suicide was utterly foreign to his nature. This contention was reinforced by Lt. Edward S. Godfrey, who, as commander of Troop K, examined Custer's body. According to Godfrey, Custer had two wounds, either of which

[6]Richard I. Dodge, *Our Wild Indians* (Hartford, 1882), 518. For support of the suicide thesis, see also Joe DeBarthe, *Life and Adventures of Frank Grouard* (St. Joseph, Mo., 1894), 262-63; and Henry Inman, *Tales of the Trail* (Topeka, 1898), 276 ff.

might have been fatal. One was in the left temple and the other to the far left of the heart—unlikely choices for a right-handed man bent upon shooting himself. Later, Godfrey recalled that there had been no powder burns around the wounds on Custer's body, and he concluded that "There was no sign for the justification of the theory, insinuation or assertion that he committed suicide."[7]

The theory that Custer killed himself was never widely accepted because it is not the kind of behavior expected of heroes. Naturally enough, the most popular version was the bloodiest. The story of how the Sioux warrior Rain-in-the-Face killed the General and then cut the heart out of his body has been chronicled in prose and verse until it represents probably the most oft-told fantasy of the Little Bighorn. Even today, belief in this tale exemplifies how prone most readers are to accept without question the truth of the printed word.

As did most other myths of the Little Bighorn, the story of Rain-in-the-Face originated with energetic newsmen who fashioned additional horrors to feed a thrill-hungry populace. A special press release from Chicago, dated July 12, 1876, announced that "Rain-in-the-Face cut the heart from Gen. Custer's body, put it on a

[7]A. J. Partoll (ed.), *After the Custer Battle* (Sources of Northwest History No. 29, Montana State University: Missoula, n.d.), 3. This leaflet is a reproduction of a letter from Godfrey to Montana artist E. S. Paxson, Jan. 16, 1896. See also Godfrey, "Custer's Last Battle," Montana Historical Society, *Contributions,* IX, 202.

pole and held a grand war dance about it."⁸ This news was repeated by most of the leading journals and rapidly spread throughout the country.

Rain-in-the-Face was singled out as the villain because of an episode in which he figured two years before the battle. During the Yellowstone Expedition of 1873, the sutler and the veterinarian of the Seventh Cavalry strayed from the command and were murdered by a roving band of Sioux. More than a year later, Rain-in-the-Face was heard boasting of this deed while drawing rations at Standing Rock Indian Agency. General Custer sent a detachment of troops under his brother, Capt. Tom Custer, to arrest the Sioux warrior. Rain-in-the-Face was lodged in the guardhouse at Fort Lincoln, but he escaped and allegedly vowed revenge on his captors. Apocryphal or not, the revenge motif made too good a story for any romanticist to overlook, although to this day it is not entirely certain that Rain-in-the-Face even participated in the Custer Fight.

The newspapers gave birth to the story, but Henry Wadsworth Longfellow immortalized it in "The Revenge of Rain-in-the-Face."

---

⁸*New York Herald*, July 13, 1876. Said Col. Henry Inman: "In all probability the story was made out of 'whole cloth' by a certain New York newspaper correspondent in whose journal it first appeared. I knew him well, and his reputation for unexaggerated truth was far from being as orthodox as he of the cherry tree fame." *Tales of the Trail*, 276.

But the foemen fled in the night
And Rain-in-the-Face, in his flight,
Uplifted high in the air
As a ghastly trophy, bore
The brave heart, that beat no more
of the White Chief with the yellow hair.

Other writers also found the details of Rain-in-the-Face's bestiality too macabre to resist. Wrote one: "Hardly had his [Custer's] brave heart ceased to beat when the savage whom he would have hanged for the murder of two helpless old men bent over him, intent upon securing some ghastly trophy of vengeance."[9] And another: "The painted, blood-begrimed demon approached the body of our beloved General, ere scarce the noble spirit had flown, and with fiendish glee *cut the heart from his body.*"[10]

Many variations of the Rain-in-the-Face tale were told and retold. Even today it frequently appears in print, despite positive evidence that General Custer's body was not mutilated. As early as July 1876, the first officer to reach the Custer Battlefield after the fight took issue with those who would magnify the already gruesome details of the action. In a long letter to a Montana newspaper, Lt. James H. Bradley described the battlefield in detail. He concluded by categorically declaring that he "was a witness to the recognition of the

[9]D. M. Kelsey, *Our Pioneer Heroes and their Daring Deeds* (San Francisco, 1888), 530.

[10]Anon., *Our Great Indian War, Mustang Bill Among the Sioux Indians* (Philadelphia, 1886), 78.

remains of Custer. Two other officers of that regiment were also present and they could not have been mistaken, and the body so identified was wholly unmutilated."[11]

In a slightly different form, the story was even more widely credited. According to this version, Rain-in-the-Face directed his ire at the remains of Capt. Tom Custer. Even the General's widow did not question this rendition. She wrote in 1885 that "The vengeance of that incarnate fiend was concentrated upon the man who had effected his capture. It was found on the battlefield that he had cut out the brave heart of that gallant, loyal, and lovable man, our brother Tom."[12]

Rain-in-the-Face himself gave the tale an appreciable stimulus while on exhibition at Coney Island in 1894. Two journalists primed him with firewater and secured the following contribution to history:

> The long sword's blood and brains splashed in my face. It felt hot, and blood ran in my mouth. I could taste it. I was mad . . . I saw Little Hair [Tom Custer]. I remembered my vow. I was crazy; I feared nothing . . . I don't know how many I killed trying to get at him. He knew me. I laughed at him. I saw his mouth move, but there was so much noise I couldn't hear his voice. He was afraid. When I got near enough I shot him with my revolver. My gun [rifle] was gone, I don't know where. I leaped from my pony and cut out his heart and bit a piece out of it and spit it in his face.

[11]*Helena Herald*, July 25, 1876, quoted in Graham, *Story of the Little Big Horn*, 163.

[12]Custer, *Boots and Saddles*, 215.

I got back on my pony and rode off shaking it. I was satisfied and sick of fighting; I didn't scalp him.[13]

The Coney Island narrative was eagerly accepted as substantiation of the early press bulletins, and more than half a century later it was still being reproduced as documented history. Less sensational was Rain-in-the-Face's testimony given virtually as a death-bed statement to Dr. Charles Eastman, himself a Sioux. Dr. Eastman interviewed the old warrior at Standing Rock Agency two months before his death in 1905. Said Rain-in-the-Face:

> Many lies have been told of me. Some say that I killed the chief, and others say that I cut the heart out of his brother, Tom Custer, because he caused me to be imprisoned. Why in that fight the excitement was so great that we scarcely recognized our nearest friends. Everything was done like lightning. After the battle we young men were chasing horses all over the prairie; and if any mutilating was done, it was by the old men.[14]

This version of the Rain-in-the-Face story is less easily disproved than the first. Tom Custer's body was frightfully mutilated, a fact that has helped to reinforce the charge against Rain-in-the-Face. However, Lieutenant Godfrey, who identified Tom's remains, did not recall that the heart was removed. Other witnesses were more specific. Capt. F. W. Benteen and Dr. H. R. Porter

---

[13]Thomas W. Kent, "The Personal Story of Rain-in-the-Face," *Outdoor Life*, XI (March, 1903); reproduced in Brady, *Indian Fights and Fighters*, 279-89.

[14]Charles A. Eastman, "Rain-in-the-Face, the Story of a Sioux Warrior," *Outlook*, Oct. 27, 1906, 507-12.

both examined Tom's body and afterward stated that the heart had not been removed.[15]

Besides Rain-in-the-Face, the fraternity of Custer slayers includes such names as Big Nose, Flat Hip, and Red Horse. Little Knife, a Hunkpapa Sioux, bestowed the laurels on a 15-year-old boy, whom he alleged shot Custer. In another story, two sons of Inkpaduta, a Santee Sioux chief, fired the fusillade that wiped out the last few soldiers, including Custer.

As recently as the spring of 1956, a magazine introduced "facts just unearthed . . . that will require a revision of most history books."[16] The article attempted to show that Custer was the first to die, not the last. Although the authors obtained their information from aged Sioux informants, the "facts just unearthed" actually appeared in the stories of Cheyenne Indians published by Grinnell as far back as 1915. These Indians told of four Cheyenne warriors who fired on Custer's command as it descended Medicine Tail Coulee toward the village, and cut down "the leader." The original story may have been true, partly true, or entirely false. If true, "the leader" may have been Custer or any other officer of the command. In any event, only the the body of

---

[15]Godfrey, "Custer's Last Battle," Montana Historical Society, *Contributions*, IX, 203; Charles F. Roe in C. E. DeLand, *The Sioux Wars*, South Dakota Historical Society, *Collections*, XV (1930), 687. In a letter to Col. W. A. Graham, Dec. 29, 1926, D. F. Barry wrote, "Gen. Benteen says he will make [an] affidavit that Tom Custer's heart was not cut out, and Dr. Porter states positively that it was not." Original in L. A. Frost collection, Monroe, Mich.

[16]Robert Crichton and David Miller, "Custer's Last Stand, Legend—or Blunder?" *Argosy*, May 1956, 19-21.

Sergeant Butler was found near this spot, while Custer's lay a full three-fourths of a mile to the north.

In 1957 Stanley Vestal, renowned historian of the Sioux, added yet another name to the aboriginal roll of Indians who killed Custer—that of the Sioux Chief White Bull.[17] According to Vestal, as the warriors broke into the little ring of troopers who had gathered around Custer for the last stand, White Bull engaged in a rousing personal encounter with the General. The two pummeled each other with their fists, and Custer even tried to bite White Bull's nose off. When Custer drew his pistol, White Bull seized it and shot the cavalryman with his own weapon. Vestal explained that White Bull personally told him this story in the early 1930's, when Vestal was gathering material for his book, *Warpath, The True Story of the Fighting Sioux*, published in 1934. Fearing that "some hothead might try to harm the old man," Vestal waited until after White Bull's death to give his secret to the world.

So rapidly have the claims multiplied that the number of "Indians who killed Custer" is now exceeded only by the number of "sole white survivors" of the battle.

Less widely publicized than most, but possessing a charm and dignity entirely foreign to the saga of Rain-in-the-Face or the claims of his successors, was the tradition recorded by Dr. Thomas B. Marquis, agency

17Stanley Vestal, "The Man Who Killed Custer," *American Heritage,* VIII (February, 1957), 4-10.

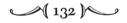

physician on the Northern Cheyenne Reservation at
Lame Deer, Montana.[18]

During his term of service at Lame Deer, Dr. Marquis received occasional intimations from the Indians
that a Southern Cheyenne named Brave Bear, who had
been in the Northern Cheyenne camp on the Little Bighorn on the day of the battle, was the Indian who shot
Custer. Following these leads, Dr. Marquis at length
succeeded in uncovering the story of Brave Bear.

During the late 1860's, when the Seventh Cavalry
was campaigning on the plains of Nebraska, Kansas,
and Indian Territory, Custer went into a camp of the
southern branch of the Cheyenne tribe, smoked the
peace pipe, and persuaded the tribal leaders to bring
their people to Fort Sill and surrender. To Indians,
smoking the pipe was a very sacred ceremony, and they
considered that Custer had thus bound himself by oath
never again to war upon the Cheyennes.

After the Battle of the Little Bighorn, the Northern
Cheyennes learned that the chief of the white soldiers
had been Custer, the same who had smoked the pipe
with their kindred in the south seven years before. Obviously, the Vast Spirit had caused the death of Long Hair
as punishment for violating the oath he had taken at
the pipe ceremony in 1869. And just as obviously, the
Vast Spirit's agent must have been someone who was
present both at the pipe ceremony and at the death
scene. Only one Indian in the entire hostile village met

[18]Thomas B. Marquis, *Which Indian Killed Custer?* (Hardin, Mont., 1933.)

these requirements—Brave Bear. Therefore, decided the tribal elders, Brave Bear must have been the Indian who killed Custer.

Marquis bided his time. Finally, in 1929, he chanced to be in a group of Indians that included Brave Bear. Conforming to Indian etiquette, Marquis broached the subject to a mutual friend, Big Beaver, and, using sign language, said, "Some white people say this man Brave Bear killed General Custer." The Indians burst into laughter. Then Big Beaver explained how Brave Bear had won his purely honorary distinction as the Indian who killed Custer. They had laughed, said Big Beaver, because the white people were taking literally the whispers they heard of Brave Bear's role in the Custer Battle. Then Big Beaver and the others repeated what Marquis had been told time and again by the Cheyennes: "None of the Indians ever knew who killed Custer. None of them even knew until long afterward that he was there."

Over the years, Custer has been killed by lance, by arrow, by tomahawk, and by bullet. He has gone down fighting with saber, with pistol, and with swinging carbine butt. He has been the first to die and the last to die. His body has been scalped and horribly mutilated, and it has been the only one left untouched—a mark of respect for a great warrior.

The foundation for the legend, as we have seen, was laid by the newspapermen of the 1870's and 1880's, many of whom were guilty of deliberate fabrication.

Legend of the Little Bighorn

Writers who followed the journalists built upon the foundation. Their methods were characterized, in greater or lesser degree, by forced interpretation, uncritical use of printed sources, uncritical acceptance of questionable testimony, and literary embellishment often approaching laughable extremes. By these methods Whittaker sought to evoke an image of Custer as a knight in shining armor whose every thought and deed was nobly inspired. By these methods Buel created what in his day passed for a stirring word picture of a gallant death struggle. And because of these methods, Rain-in-the-Face found himself the villain of a grotesque drama that sprang from a brief press bulletin dreamed up by a frontier correspondent with an active imagination. To such literary irresponsibility the Custer legend owes its longevity and its prominent place among the myths that abound in American history from Columbus to MacArthur. But whereas George Washington long ago relinquished his hatchet, and Barbara Frietchie finally retired to her sick-bed, George Custer rides up Battle Ridge year after year to a newly reconstructed death.

✗ ✗ ✗

The number of "only survivors" of Custer's Last Stand long ago exceeded the full strength of Custer's battalion, and the number continues to grow each year. A few of the only survivor stories are well reasoned and based on wide knowledge of facts and probabilities, although none has ever proved flawless; the overwhelming majority, however, are so wildly unrelated to known reality that they command contempt from even the imperfectly informed student. Yet the fact remains that over a score of Custer's men were never accounted for, and the very real possibility exists that someone did indeed escape from the ridge of death. But so tangled and so fruitful of conflicting interpretations is the evidence that no claimant or his historical executor is ever likely to win endorsement from the ruthlessly skeptical jurors who will sit in judgment on the claim.

To examine the ridiculous claims would be pointless; to examine the serious ones would require long and complex lines of logic that, under the scrutiny of experts, would with relentless certainty break down at one point or another. There is one claim, however, that deserves attention. It is the most persistent and popular, and indeed it is not without a certain indirect merit. We shall examine what legend says happened, and speculate upon what in truth may have happened.

The first press accounts of the Custer Battle revealed that "only one Crow scout remained to tell the tale." His name was Curley, and he had turned up at the mouth of the Little Bighorn, where the steamer *Far West* lay moored to the bank, at noon on June 28. "He was terribly cast down and excited," wrote the correspondent, "but could not make himself understood. Finally he took a piece of paper and pencil, and drawing a fair sketch of the battle as it afterwards proved, and in rude figures a few soldiers [told about the fight]."

Legend of the Little Bighorn

Curley did in fact arrive on the *Far West*. Sgt. James Wilson of the Engineers recorded in his diary the appearance of Curley on the vessel. He wore an "exceedingly dejected countenance," but his appetite was "in first rate order." He was visibly affected by emotion, and, although unable to speak English, managed by drawing a rude diagram, accompanied by pantomime, to convey the news that Custer had suffered a serious reverse.[19]

Starting from these simple facts, the correspondent now began to embroider: "The Crow Indian who managed to escape did so by rushing to the river and washing off his paint, and changing the dress of his hair, and putting on a Sioux blanket, charged with the Sioux, escaping, however, when an opportunity presented."[20] By the time Whittaker published his *Life of Custer*, Curley's escape, as we have already seen (p. 123), had taken on added drama. He offered to lead Custer to safety, but the General, after pondering a moment, declined, preferring to die with his men. In another version, Curley slit open the belly of a dead horse and hid inside the carcass until the Sioux vacated the field.

The Curley story, especially the blanket version, promptly won a secure place in the literature of the Little Bighorn, and has been tiresomely chronicled in articles and books ever since. One such repetition, in a 1948 issue of *Life*, provoked an explosion from Col. W.

[19]*New York Times*, July 7, 1876; Report of Sgt. James Wilson in Report of the Secretary of War, 1877, II, 1379. See also Hanson, *Conquest of the Missouri*, 274-80, who erroneously gives the date of Curley's arrival as June 27.

[20]*New York Times*, July 9, 1876; *New York Herald*, July 26, 1876.

A. Graham. "Blankets were definitely not the Indians' summer costume," he wrote, "and the 'disguise' as a means of distracting attention, would have been as effective as a stovepipe hat and evening cape among a horde of one piece bathing suits."[21]

So deeply imbedded are the Curley myths in the legend of the Little Bighorn that it is now difficult to evaluate Curley's genuine role in the battle. Nevertheless, with the exception of one time lapse, it is possible to follow him fairly closely from the beginning of the fight to his arrival at the *Far West*.

When Terry, Gibbon, and Custer mapped out the campaign plan aboard the *Far West* on June 21, the problem of Indian scouts arose. Terry's Arikaras were from Dakota and did not know the Rosebud country. Gibbon therefore offered to lend Custer six Crow scouts under the half-breed, Mitch Bouyer. They were Half-Yellow-Face, White Swan, Hairy Moccasin, Goes Ahead, White-Man-Runs-Him, and Curley. The last, Curley, was a lad of 17, whose Indian name was Shuh-Shee-Ahsh, the son of Inside-the-Mouth and Strikes-by-the-Side-of-the-Water. With the others, he had joined Gibbon's scout detachment, commanded by Lt. James H. Bradley, at Stillwater, Montana, early in April, and had served Gibbon creditably for the past two months.[22]

21Graham to Editors of *Life*, Aug. 25, 1948. *Life* did not print the letter. Copy furnished by Colonel Graham.

22John Gibbon, "Last Summer's Campaign Against the Sioux," *American Catholic Quarterly Review*, II, 6 (April, 1877), 293; biographical data on Curley from files of the Crow Indian Agency, Mont.

Legend of the Little Bighorn

During the three-day march up the Rosebud, Custer profitably employed the Crows' knowledge of the country. When the regiment deployed for the attack on June 25, Half-Yellow-Face and White Swan remained with Reno. Hairy Moccasin, Goes Ahead, White-Man-Runs-Him, and Curley accompanied Custer. As Reno crossed the Little Bighorn to advance against the hostile camp, Custer turned right and struck north toward the lower end of the village. His four Crows, with Mitch Bouyer, rode to the left front, ascending the gentle slope that led to the bluffs above the Little Bighorn. Here, where Reno later laid out his defense perimeter, the scouts saw the Sioux village below them, and must have watched Reno collide with the enemy warriors.[23]

The Crows rode north along the rim of the bluffs. The troops, who had been paralleling the bluffs some distance to the east and well below the skyline, turned into a ravine that diverged from the line of bluffs toward Medicine Tail Coulee. About a quarter of a mile south of Medicine Tail, where the escarpment begins tapering down to the ford, the Crows halted. Although their narratives are vague in detail, it is clear from their combined import that Curley was no longer with them. Presumably he had joined Custer.

[23]Narrative of Hairy Moccasin, *Teepee Book*, II, 6 (June, 1916), 54-55; White-Man-Runs-Him in *ibid.*, 52, and in Joseph K. Dixon, *The Vanishing Race* (New York, 1913), 154-57; Goes Ahead in *ibid.*, 165-68, and in O. G. Libby, *The Arikara Narrative of the Campaign Against the Hostile Dakotas*. North Dakota Historical Society, *Collections*, VI (1920), 259-60. Lieutenant Varnum, on the left flank of Reno's line advancing down the valley, caught a fleeting glimpse of the Gray Horse Troop on the bluffs at this point. See his testimony in Graham, *Reno Court of Inquiry*. 134.

Mitch Bouyer saw that the battle would soon begin. He told the three remaining Crows that Custer did not expect them to fight, and directed them to return to the pack train. Bouyer rode to join Custer. Goes Ahead, Hairy Moccasin, and White-Man-Runs-Him lingered long enough to watch Custer go into action against the Sioux vanguard crossing the river at the ford. In a parting gesture of defiance, they discharged several volleys into the nearest tepees across the river, then retraced their path to the south. On Reno Hill they found the Major's shattered battalion, which the Sioux had just driven from the valley, and joined the detachment of Arikara scouts.[24]

But what had happened to Curley? Since his recorded interviews are muddled, it is necessary largely to discount his own testimony on time, place, and movement.[25] The late Russell White Bear, an unofficial historian of the Crows and a confidant of the Crow scouts,

[24]That night, June 25, Goes Ahead, White-Man-Runs-Him, and Hairy Moccasin left Reno Hill and rode north. They met Gibbon's column next morning marching up the Bighorn, and managed to convey the impression that Custer had met with disaster, although this was generally disbelieved by the officers. The three badly frightened scouts continued to their agency at Stillwater. Gibbon, "Last Summer's Campaign," 294-95; James H. Bradley, *Journal of the Campaign Against the Hostile Dakota in 1876 under Command of General John Gibbon*, Montana Historical Society, *Contributions*, II (1896), 220. Half-Yellow-Face remained to care for White Swan, who had been wounded, and later moved him with the rest of Reno's wounded to the *Far West*. Gibbon, "Hunting Sitting Bull," 674.

[25]*Army and Navy Journal*, Aug. 5, 1876; interview with Lt. C. F. Roe at Fort Custer, *Army and Navy Journal*, March 25, 1882; Dixon, *Vanishing Race*, 160-63; *Teepee Book*, June 1916, 56; Roe in *Motor Travel*, June-Aug., 1926, reproduced in part in DeLand, *Sioux Wars*, 684. The field notes of W. M. Camp in the possession of Mrs. R. S. Ellison contain Curley interviews that might prove of greater value than the published versions.

stated that Curley accompanied Custer to the point on Medicine Tail Coulee where the main command separated from the Gray Horse Troop (E), which continued some distance down the coulee; here he turned around and rode back in the direction from which the battalion had come.[26] It is the consensus that, in order to have conveyed as much information about the battle as he did, he must have witnessed part of the fighting. From what distance may never be known.[27] In this, his distinction is no greater than the other three Crows, for they, too, observed some of the action before returning to Reno.

Curley joined a Ree scout named Black Fox somewhere in the vicinity of Reno Hill in the late afternoon or early evening of June 25. Black Fox told Curley he could show him where the soldiers had left some hard bread, and the two Indians retraced the trail of the Seventh Cavalry back across the Wolf Mountains to near the campsite of the night before. Here they parted, Curley vowing that he was going home.[28] He crossed to the headwaters of Tullock's Creek and descended to its mouth, then rode to the mouth of the Bighorn, arriving on the morning of June 26.

[26]Quoted in Fred Dustin, *The Custer Tragedy* (Ann Arbor, Mich., 1939), x.

[27]In four separate accounts, only two of which are published, Curley gave evidence that he witnessed the fight of the Gray Horse Troop in the ravine southwest of Custer Hill. For discussion of this, see Kuhlman, *Legend into History*, 237-39.

[28]Narrative of Red Star (confirmed by Goes Ahead), in Libby, *Arikara Narrative*, 119-20. These Indians met the pack train descending Reno Creek and told the officers Custer was beaten. Testimony of Lt. E. G. Mathey, in charge of the pack train, in Graham, *Reno Court of Inquiry*, 458.

Thomas LeForge, Gibbon's interpreter, had taken ill
and had been left behind at a military hospital on the
north bank of the Yellowstone across from the mouth of
the Bighorn. That morning he saw Curley preparing
breakfast on the other bank and signed to him across the
river. Curley asked where Gray Beard (Gibbon) was and,
on being told, mounted his horse and rode up the Bighorn. He was next seen at the mouth of the Little Bighorn
at noon on the 28th. It is a mystery where he was and
what he did between the morning of the 26th and noon
of the 28th, when he boarded the *Far West*. He probably
slept part of the time, for he had travelled all the night
preceding.[29]

Curley could not speak English in 1876, and only
acquired a broken knowledge of it in later years. Consequently, it was difficult for him to refute the romantic
stories of his escape from the Custer Fight. He was interviewed by Lt. James H. Bradley, through Interpreter
LeForge, at the mouth of the Bighorn a short time later.
As LeForge recalled it for Marquis:

> I interpreted for Lieutenant Bradley when he inter-
> viewed Curley several days after the Custer Battle . . .
> again and again during the long examination of him by
> Bradley, the young scout said, "I was not in the fight."
> When gazed upon and congratulated by visitors, he de-
> clared, "I did nothing wonderful; I was not in it." He told
> us that when the engagement opened he was behind, with

29Thomas B. Marquis, *Memoirs of a White Crow Indian* (New York,
1928), 247-48. Curley gave LeForge no intimation that a fight had occurred,
afterward explaining that he was so sleepy that he thought everyone knew
about it.

other Crows. He hurried away to a distance of about a mile, paused there, and looked for a brief time upon the conflict. Soon he got still farther away, stopping on a hill to take another look.[30]

But mere denial could not stop the story. Whittaker picked it up from the newspapers, and one popular writer after another, copying Whittaker, repeated it. Pretty soon Curley quit denying it, for no one would believe him and the notoriety was not entirely disagreeable. His people knew the truth, and they called him a liar. So did the Sioux, who naturally did not like to think that anyone had escaped. At the Tenth Anniversary observance in 1886, Chief Gall called Curley a liar to his face.[31] But Curley won in the end. He enjoyed a wider reputation than any of the tribesmen who scorned him, and when he was finally laid to rest in the Custer Battlefield National Cemetery in 1923 his name descended to posterity as an integral part of the Custer legend, the only survivor of Custer's Last Stand.

✗   ✗   ✗

But there really was an only survivor whose claim no one disputes—Comanche, the claybank charger that bore Capt. Myles W. Keogh. On the morning of June 27, as the burial parties completed their grim task, Lt. Henry J. Nowlan discovered Comanche wandering over

[30]*Ibid.*, 250-51.

[31]Usher L. Burdick (ed.), *David F. Barry's Indian Notes on the Custer Battle* (Baltimore, 1937), 7. David F. Barry, famous western photographer, was present at the ceremony, and recorded the events of the observance in his notes.

the battlefield. The horse was so pocked with arrow and bullet wounds that he was given little chance to live. But the awareness that he was probably the sole survivor of Custer's command prompted the men to spare him.[32]

Lieutenant Nowlan had Comanche's wounds dressed, and the horse was tenderly moved to the steamer *Far West*. On the stern of the vessel a stall was erected and bedded with grass. His "care and welfare became the special duty of the whole boat's company."[33] Comanche was brought to Fort Lincoln, where another special stall, complete with sling, was built. He remained suspended for a year while Blacksmith Gustave Korn and Pvt. John Burkman, Custer's former orderly, nursed the wounded animal back to health.[34]

On April 10, 1878, the regimental commander, Col. S. D. Sturgis, issued General Order No. 10, in which he directed that a special stall be designated for Comanche, that he should never be ridden nor put to any kind of work, and that on all ceremonial occasions he should be led, in saddle and bridle with reversed boots, by a

[32]Luce, *Keogh, Comanche and Custer*, 64-65. Capt. Thomas McDougall of B Troop stated in a letter to Gen. E. S. Godfrey, May 18, 1909, that he discovered Comanche in some brush near the river. Copy furnished by Col. W. A. Graham.

[33]Hanson, *Conquest of the Missouri*, 206.

[34]Luce, *Keogh, Comanche and Custer*, 66. John Burkman—"Old Neutriment"—was Custer's devoted orderly. He was with the pack train on June 25, 1876, but so bleak was life without his adored commander that he regretted ever after having been left behind. In 1925 he took his own life and was buried on the Custer Battlefield in the national cemetery. Glendolin D. Wagner, *Old Neutriment* (Boston, 1934).

mounted trooper of Keogh's old Troop I in formation.[35]
Comanche took full advantage of his prerogatives and
wandered amiably around the post flaunting his privi-
leged position. Lovingly cared for by Blacksmith Korn,
the horse became a symbol of that destructive hour on
the Little Bighorn. Fifteen years after the battle, Comanche had won the affectionate rank of the Seventh's
"second commanding officer." But after Korn's death at
Wounded Knee in 1890, Comanche began to fail. Wrote
his biographer:

> From the date of Comanche's return to Fort Riley (Jan-
> uary 26, 1891) he seemed to have but little interest in life.
> He just "didn't care." No matter what Pete Wey [his new
> attendant] tried to do for him, Comanche seemed to get
> more morose. His "sanitary inspection" of the garbage cans
> became more frequent. His "sprees" at the canteen [Co-
> manche was an inveterate beer-drinker] almost developed
> a "panhandle" status. After such "sprees" he was content
> to lie in his stall or mud wallows until finally on November
> 6, 1891, he passed away at the age of twenty-nine years.[36]

But Comanche only died physically. His spirit is still
part and parcel of the traditions of the Seventh Cavalry,
one of the few uncolored parts of the vast legend of the
Little Bighorn. And he is still there for all to see,
mounted and displayed in a glass case in the Dyche
Museum at the University of Kansas.

---

[35]Quoted in Luce, *Keogh, Comanche and Custer*, 67.
[36]*Ibid.*, 77.

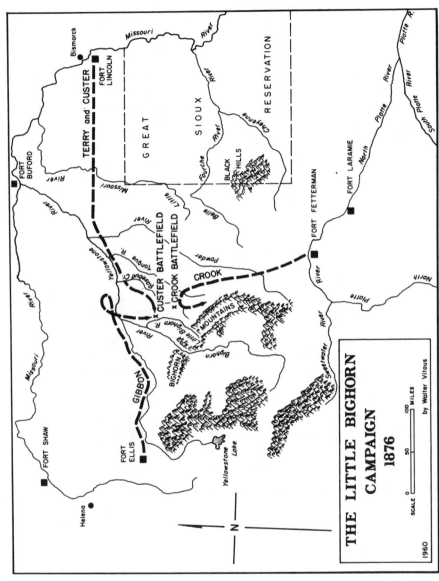

THE LITTLE BIGHORN
CAMPAIGN
1876

by Walter Vitous

1960

SCALE 0   50   100
              MILES

Chapter VI

BIBLIOGRAPHICAL SURVEY, 1876-1900

IT WOULD BE AN IMPOSSIBLE task to compile an exhaustive bibliography of Little Bighorn literature. The late Fred Dustin made a manful attempt, and the result is as complete a bibliography as is ever likely to be assembled. First published in 1939 in his book, *The Custer Tragedy*, it was later revised to include additions up to the end of 1952. This revision was included in Col. W. A. Graham's *The Custer Myth* in 1953. Although the annotations reflect Dustin's hatred of Custer, the bibliography is a monumental work and an indispensable tool for the student of the Little Bighorn. The following essay is in no sense an attempt to equal or surpass Dustin's accomplishment. Rather, it is designed to fill in some of the gaps in the evolution of the Custer Controversy left by the topical approach of the preceding chapters. It focuses on the quarter-century following the battle, for that is when the Custer Controversy was born. The titles issued since the turn of the century are so numerous that, for this· period, only a brief consideration of the men who most fundamentally influenced interpretations will be attempted.

X   X   X

CONTRIBUTIONS BY PARTICIPANTS IN THE CAMPAIGN

The role of the newspapers in the historiography of the Custer Fight was not entirely sinister. They also made some important contributions to the sources of Little Bighorn history. Correspondents interviewed participants in the battle; and in addition to these accounts the papers printed articles penned by officers of the Montana column. Major Brisbin's supplement to Mark Kellogg's journal is the outstanding example of the latter (see p. 31). Of the former, the accounts of Capt. F. W. Benteen, Lt. C. C. DeRudio, Maj. M. A. Reno, Dr. H. R. Porter, scout George Herendeen, and Pvt. John Dolan of M Troop are notable.[1] Although historians have made little use of these accounts, they merit serious study, for they were recorded before angry partisanship had warped memories.

The Congressional documents of 1876 and 1877 also contain important first-hand material. Besides the official reports of Terry, Gibbon, Reno, and Benteen, a

[1]Benteen in *New York Herald*, Aug. 8, 1876; DeRudio in *ibid.*, July 30, 1876 and *Chicago Times*, Aug. 2, 1876; Reno in *New York Herald*, Aug. 8, 1876; Porter in *ibid.*, July 11, 1876; Herendeen in *ibid.*, July 8, 1876; and Dolan in *ibid.*, July 23, 1876.

number of diaries kept by members of the expedition were reproduced. The report of Lt. Edward Maguire, Chief Engineer, Department of Dakota, was not submitted in time for inclusion in the Secretary of War's Report for 1876, and was published the following year. In addition to his personal day-by-day journal, Maguire included the journals of Lt. George D. Wallace, itinerist of the Custer column, which covers the march up the Rosebud, June 21 to 24; the journal of Lt. E. J. McClernand, Gibbon's chief engineer officer, covering the entire period the Montana column was in the field, April 1 to September 29; and the journal of Sgt. James E. Wilson, one of Maguire's enlisted engineers, who was on the *Far West*.[2]

In 1877 Col. John Gibbon set down his recollections of the 1876 campaign and contributed them, in two installments, to the *American Catholic Quarterly Review*. Gibbon was a close observer and recalled many details that escaped the memory of others. Both articles contain important material. Especially valuable is the account of his inspection of the Custer Battlefield on the morning of June 28.[3]

In 1892 there appeared a little volume from the pen of Frances Chamberlain Holley entitled *Once Their Home*. Mrs. Holley's interpretations of the battle resem-

[2]The official reports of Gibbon, Terry, Reno, and Benteen are in Report of the Secretary of War, 1876, Vol. I; the journals in Report of the Chief of Engineers, Vol. II of Report of the Secretary of War, 1877, 1376 ff.

[3]"Last Summer's Expedition Against the Sioux," and "Hunting Sitting Bull," in the April and October issues.

ble many other outpourings of the day, but she applied herself more diligently to obtaining first-hand material than did most of her contemporaries. She won contributions from several participants in the battle whose testimony is available nowhere else but the Reno Court of Inquiry record. These were Capt. Thomas H. McDougall, Lt. Luther R. Hare, and Lt. Charles A. Varnum. Additional narratives by Dr. H. R. Porter, George Herendeen, and Fred Gerard, whose stories are available elsewhere, were likewise included.[4]

Gerard's account in this book contained remarks bearing on Custer's departure from Terry's campaign plan. Gerard wrote that, when the Seventh marched up the Rosebud on June 22, he remained behind to pick up some dispatches. He was standing beside Terry and Capt. E. W. Smith awaiting instructions when he overheard Terry remark to Smith, "Custer is happy now, off with a roving command of fifteen days! I told him if he found any Indians not to do as Reno did, but if he thought he could whip them to do so!" Fred Dustin believed this too neat a story. Gerard hated Reno, Dustin pointed out, because Reno had once discharged him as interpreter during an absence of Custer. Gerard's story was also published by the North Dakota Historical Society in Vol. I of its *Collections* (1906).

We have had occasion several times in this work to note the article of Capt. Edward S. Godfrey in *Century*

4Frances C. Holley, *Once Their Home* (Chicago, 1892) ; Varnum, 242-44; McDougall, 244-46; Hare, 247; Porter, 247-49; Herendeen, 249-50; Gerard, 262-66.

Magazine for January 1892. Godfrey's hatred of Reno exceeded his dislike of Custer. Although he shaded his article somewhat in Custer's favor, he wrote probably the most dispassionate, comprehensive, and sound account of the battle to appear before 1900, and his influence on later writers is distinctly apparent. In later years he fell under the spell of Mrs. Custer, and his 1923 article in the Montana Historical Society *Contributions* is more biased and less valuable.

The second volume of the Montana Historical Society's *Contributions* appeared in 1896. It included the journal of Lt. James H. Bradley, Gibbon's chief of scouts, covering the period of Gibbon's field operations up to June 26, unhappily the stage of preparation for publication at which Bradley laid down his work to participate in the Nez Percé campaign of 1877. He was killed at the Battle of the Big Hole. The journal exhibits the attention to detail of a trained historian. It has recently been made more widely available as a separate volume.[5] Vol. II of the *Contributions* also contains the diary of Matthew Carroll, civilian wagon master in the Gibbon column, but it is quite brief.

In 1900 Robert Vaughn, early pioneer of western Montana, published his recollections of the history of Montana, and set down the stories of Billy Jackson and George Herendeen, both civilians who fought under Reno in the valley and on the bluffs.[6]

[5] James H. Bradley, *The March of the Montana Column: A Prelude to the Custer Disaster,* ed. by Edgar I. Stewart (Norman, 1961).

[6] Robert Vaughn, *Then and Now* (Minneapolis, 1900), 310-15.

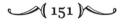

Custer and the Great Controversy

In 1877 Mrs. Frances Fuller Victor, one of Hubert Howe Bancroft's many assistants, published a history of the mountain men who ranged the Bighorn Mountains during the fur trade era,[7] and added a supplement of 156 pages dealing with the later Indian wars of the region. Her treatment of the Custer Battle was well done, impartial, and usually let the official reports and contemporary testimony as it appeared in the newspapers tell the story. She recounted the Curley story substantially as related by Whittaker, but this legend was to be almost unanimously accepted by writers for many years to come. She seemed inclined to defend Reno and, without naming him, mildly challenged Whittaker's partisanship.

Mrs. Victor was the first of several writers of the period to reprint the estimate of Custer "by a gentleman who accompanied General Custer on his Yellowstone expedition," which first appeared in the *New York Tribune*. The "gentleman" was Capt. William Ludlow, then acting as chief engineer officer of the department. Ludlow's appraisal was unbiased, and constitutes a fair attempt by one not involved in the later partisanship to analyze and evaluate Custer's character.[8]

[7]Frances Fuller Victor, *Eleven Years in the Rocky Mountains* (Hartford, 1877).

[8]Also reproduced in T. M. Newson, *Thrilling Scenes Among the Indians* (New York, 1884), 174-77, and W. Fletcher Johnson, *Life of Sitting Bull* (n. p., 1891), 132-34.

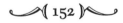

Bibliographical Survey

In 1879 Gen. Henry B. Carrington, who commanded
Fort Phil Kearny at the time of the Fetterman disaster
(see p. 77), published the fifth edition of the journal
kept by his late wife during their service on the Bozeman Trail in 1866-67.[9] Carrington, who was then building a second career as a professor of history at Wabash
College, Indiana, appended a history of Indian affairs
on the plains from 1867 to 1877. It was constructed pri-
marily from official reports and his own memory. Somewhat sympathetic to Custer, Carrington nevertheless
indulged in no personalities, and more or less accepted
General Sherman's analysis of the Custer Fight (see p.
45).

A semi-official publication was issued by the Government Printing Office in 1882 under General Sheridan's
name.[10] It was a year-by-year recital of every engagement, from skirmish to full-scale battle, between U. S.
troops and hostile Indians in the Military Division of the
Missouri for the period between 1868 and 1882. It was
compiled entirely from the records on file at division
headquarters in Chicago, and the result was a dry nar-
ration of fact without any attempt to explain the reasons
for the Custer disaster in terms of personalities. Nevertheless, it is of supreme value to the student of the era.

Probably the most thorough and scholarly history of
the Custer Battle to appear between 1876 and 1900 is

[9]Margaret Irving and Henry B. Carrington, *Absaraka, Land of Massacre*
(Philadelphia, 1879).

[10]Philip H. Sheridan, *Record of Engagements with Hostile Indians within
the Military Division of the Missouri from* 1868-1882 (Washington, 1882).

to be found in a history of the Indian wars bearing the forbidding title *Massacres of the Mountains,* by Jacob P. Dunn. His treatment of the battle and its controversy is accurate, fair, and impartial. Shrewdly appraising the bitter partisanship, he remarked that "there has been injustice done to all the officers engaged in the battle, and it has arisen chiefly from the efforts of themselves or their friends to evade the supposed fault in the affair. There was not fairly any fault in it."[11]

The voluminous *Works* of Hubert Howe Bancroft deal with the Custer Battle in a footnote, but one several pages long. Relying on a cursory study of the official reports and newspaper accounts, Bancroft succumbed to the pitfalls involved in any attempt to treat with this subject without thorough study. The result is gross inaccuracy, the general tenor of which is suggested by his assertion that, "The little that is known of Custer's fatal fight was related to Gen. Terry . . . by a half-breed Crow scout, called Curley . . . who escaped by drawing a blanket about him after the manner of the Sioux."[12]

Prof. James P. Boyd, biographer of Grant, Sherman, Sheridan, Blaine, Harrison, and McKinley, also published a history of the Indian wars of North America.

[11] Jacob Piatt Dunn, *Massacres of the Mountains* (New York, 1886), 623. Dunn was born in Lawrenceburg, Ind., in 1855, received his BS and MS degrees from Earlham College and his LLB from the University of Michigan. An author and historian of note, he served as secretary of the Indiana Historical Society and as state librarian, as an editorial writer for the *Indianapolis Sentinel*, and as city comptroller of Indianapolis. At the time of his death in 1924 he was private secretary to Senator S. M. Ralston.

[12] Hubert H. Bancroft, *History of Washington, Idaho and Montana, 1845-1889* (Vol. XXXI of *Works*, San Francisco, 1890), 715.

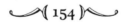

Issued twice under different titles, the work contains a chapter on the Little Bighorn which throws most of the responsibility for the disaster on Major Reno, who "was no doubt, imposed upon by Indian strategy," and whose "retreat to the bluffs was, to say the least of it, premature." Boyd softened his judgment a bit by conjecturing that, in the final reckoning, Reno probably could not have broken through to join Custer anyway.[13]

Edward S. Ellis, high school teacher and author of several history texts and the Deerfoot series of juveniles, in 1892 published an exhaustive history of the American Indian wars from Jamestown to Wounded Knee.[14] The Little Bighorn was reconstructed through the medium of Chief Gall, his narrative as printed in the *Army and Navy Journal* (see p. 107-110) being reproduced in full. The history of Comanche, the genuine "only survivor," was dealt with at length.

✗   ✗   ✗

BRANCHES FROM THE WHITTAKER TRUNK

A large number of books appeared during the period between 1876 and 1900 whose origin is to be found in Whittaker's *Life of Custer*. It was a time of widespread literary piracy. Although a few writers attempted to conceal their method beneath a veneer of shuffled sequence and wording, many simply copied the *Life*

---

[13]James P. Boyd, *Recent Indian Wars Under the Lead of Sitting Bull* (n.p., 1891), 150; *Red Men on the War Path* (n.p., 1895), 150.

[14]Edward Ellis, *The Indian Wars of the United States* (New York, 1892).

word for word. In no offspring of the *Life* is it difficult to detect the Whittaker influence. Although Whittaker's ideas have been dealt with at length, further illustration of his impact upon his contemporaries may prove revealing.

John Hanson Beadle, celebrated dime novelist, completed *Western Wilds and the Men Who Redeem Them* in 1877 and published it in 1881. Although devoting most of his energy to assailing the Mormon Church, he found space to insert an account of the Custer Fight. The following passage suggests the character of the whole: "Then Rain-in-the-Face . . . gathered his most trusty followers for a hand to hand charge. Custer fought like a tiger. With blood streaming from half a dozen gaping wounds, he killed or disabled three of the enemy with his saber, and when his last support was gone, as he lunged desperately at his nearest enemy, Rain-in-the-Face kept his oath and shot the heroic commander dead."[15] Comparison of this quotation with its counterpart in Whittaker reveals the similarities: ". . . the Indians made a hand to hand charge in which Custer fought like a tiger . . . he killed or wounded three Indians with his saber, and . . . as he ran the last man through, Rain-in-the-Face kept his oath and shot Custer."[16]

E. G. Cattermole's *Famous Frontiersmen, Pioneers and Scouts*, published in 1884, contained a biography of

---

[15]John H. Beadle, *Western Wilds and the Men who Redeem Them* (Cincinnati, 1881), 570.

[16]Whittaker, *Life of Custer*, 601.

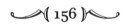

Bibliographical Survey

Custer that condensed Whittaker's *Life;*[17] while D. M. Kelsey's *Our Pioneer Heroes and their Daring Deeds,* also including a lengthy biography of Custer, exhibits probably the most striking plagiarism of Whittaker to be found.[18]

In 1881 J. W. Buel plundered Whittaker for *Heroes of the Plains,* a quote from which has been included in an earlier chapter (see p. 124). Much of the book deals with Buffalo Bill Cody, who himself undertook a literary career of sorts, in 1889 publishing *Story of the Wild West and Camp-Fire Chats.* Cody collaborated with Col. Henry Inman in *The Great Salt Lake Trail,* which appeared in 1898. All three books, dashed off hastily and with scant regard for accuracy, were designed for popular consumption. All three carried precisely the same narrative of the Custer Battle. Whether Buel wrote it and Cody plagiarized it in the two books bearing his name, or whether Cody wrote it for Buel's use and then reproduced it in subsequent years, is not known. The treatment of the Little Bighorn is highly innacurate, critical of Reno and Benteen, and eulogistic of Custer.[19]

These few samples from a vast array of Custer literature demonstrate in a modest way the profound influ-

17E. G. Cattermole, *Famous Frontiersmen, Pioneers and Scouts* (2nd ed., Tarrytown, N.Y., 1926). The first edition was published in 1884.

18D. M. Kelsey. *Our Pioneer Heroes and their Daring Deeds* (San Francisco, 1888).

19Buel, *Heroes of the Plains,* 363-99; W. F. Cody, *Story of the Wild West and Camp-Fire Chats* (Philadelphia, 1889), 664-73; Henry Inman and W. F. Cody, *The Great Salt Lake Trail* (New York, 1898), 436-42. For an interesting exercise in literary detective work on the two Cody books, see Don Russell, *The Lives and Legends of Buffalo Bill* (Norman, 1960), 146-47.

ence of the crusading novelist, Frederick Whittaker, upon the development of Custer historiography during its first quarter-century. With so many literary descendants, it is not surprising that the historical inaccuracies, and the interpretations based upon them, which appear in Custer's first biography were repeated to such an extent that they became self-perpetuating.

✗   ✗   ✗

MISCELLANEOUS

1. Judson Elliot Walker, *Campaigns of General Custer in the Northwest and the Final Surrender of Sitting Bull* (New York, 1881) is a curious mixture of poorly written and disorganized fact and fiction strongly tinctured with Whittaker, but incorporating observations of the author, a Bismarck merchant in 1876. Despite its doubtful reliability, it has been widely used as a reference work, and excerpts were selected for inclusion in Vol. IX of *America* (New York, 1925). Walker presents the results of personal interviews with many of the surrendered hostiles, including Sitting Bull, Gall, and Crow King. With the exception of the last, these interviews are unsatisfactory.

2. E. S. Topping, *Chronicles of the Yellowstone* (St. Paul, 1883), was written by a Montana pioneer of the Yellowstone country. Although his sources are not apparent, he constructed the book with more than the usual care. It was Topping's opinion that Custer was killed near the beginning of the fight, "for his proverbial pres-

ence of mind and skill in handling men in critical places, would have guided the command to a position from which an organized resistance could have been made." (pp. 187-88.) He was critical of Reno, who, he said, could easily have held his position in the timber (p. 192).

3. T. M. Newsome, *Thrilling Scenes Among the Indians* (New York, 1884), is a distressing little work that places the battle on Rosebud Creek instead of the Little Bighorn. Newsome's depiction of the last of the battle is, however, worth quoting: "All is still! All was gone! Three hundred men! hundreds of horses! the most gallant cavalry officer America ever produced passed out of life, out of activity, out of reality, down into the shadow of death!" (p. 187.)

4. Elizabeth B. Custer, *Boots and Saddles, or Life in the Dakotas with General Custer* (New York, 1885). The first of a trio of reminiscences covering plains life with her husband, Mrs. Custer here writes of their experiences during three years in Dakota. She avoids the painful subject of the last battle, but vividly pictures the prophetic scene in her home on June 25, at the hour of the battle. The primary value of the book for students of the Little Bighorn lies in an appendix reproducing in part the letters received from her husband on the last march. The General was a prodigious letter writer, and Mrs. Custer includes eight, the first dated May 20, 46 miles west of Fort Lincoln, the last at the mouth of the Rosebud on the morning of June 22.

5. Joseph Henry Taylor, *Sketches of Frontier and Indian Life on the Upper Missouri and Great Plains* (Potts-
town, Pa., 1889; Washburn, N.D., 1895; Bismarck, 1897).
This popular little volume of frontier impressions went
through three editions, but for purposes of the Little Bighorn contains nothing of importance except interesting,
if flowery, sketches of Charley Reynolds and Mark Kellogg. As a collector's item, however, the book, especially
the first edition, is extremely valuable.

6. John F. Finerty, *War-Path and Bivouac, or the
Conquest of the Sioux* (New York, 1890). Correspondent
for the *Chicago Times* with General Crook's column,
Finerty made an important contribution to the sources of
the Indian wars, but his account of the Little Bighorn,
highly flavored with sensationalism, is second-hand and
loaded with errors.

7. W. Fletcher Johnson, *Life of Sitting Bull* (n.p.,
1891). Johnson hastily rushed this work into print to capitalize on popular interest in the death of Sitting Bull
and the Ghost Dance outbreak of 1890. The result is un-
even, although reproduction of Captain Ludlow's estimate of Custer and the story written by Major Brisbin
to supplement the Mark Kellogg notes makes these
contemporary newspaper stories more readily available.

8. Henry Davenport Northrup, *Indian Horrors, or
Massacres by the Red Men* (Oakland, Calif., 1891), is
novel in censuring all three commanders—Custer for
being "too rash and intrepid," Reno for lacking the "vet-
eran courage of Custer and his men," and Benteen for

being "culpably and inexcusably tardy" in advancing to Custer's aid (pp. 406-7, 413). The story of a white scout named Ridgley, one of the legion of white prisoners literature places in the Sioux village, is also included.

9. Alexander Berghold, *The Indian's Revenge, or Days of Horror* (San Francisco, 1891), is another collector's item, published also in German in 1891 under the title of *Indianer-Rache*. Its contents offer nothing worthy of remark, except that the Custer Battle was fought in the Black Hills.

10. Joe DeBarthe, *The Life and Adventures of Frank Grouard* (St. Joseph, Mo., 1894), is the autobiography of Crook's chief of scouts. It contains some material that is quite good, but historians have always doubted the proposition that Grouard, at Crook's base camp on Goose Creek, 75 miles to the south, learned from Indian smoke signals of the Custer disaster on the morning of June 25 and was on the battlefield that night. Aside from the obvious difficulty that Grouard learned of the fight several hours before it began, there is no evidence to suggest that anyone in Crook's camp knew of the battle until July 10, when Louis Richard and Ben Arnold brought the word from Fort Fetterman. Edited by Edgar I. Stewart, the book was republished in 1958. Stewart remarks that the Grouard story could well be true, although occurring on the 26th instead of the 25th (p. 123, note 2).

11. J. Lee Humfreville, *Twenty Years Among our Savage Indians* (Hartford, 1897), is the reminiscence of

a retired quartermaster captain with eight years of frontier service. He informs us that so competent an officer as Custer could not have erred in dividing his command had he not been badly advised by incompetent scouts. Otherwise, the account follows Godfrey and an interview with Rain-in-the-Face.

12. Elbridge S. Brooks, *The Master of the Strong Hearts* (New York, 1898). This is boys' fiction, but the self-proclaimed historians of the period could have learned some lessons from it. Excepting the Rain-in-the-Face myth and certain liberties recognized as legitimate for historical novels, this book is one of the best popular histories of the day.

13. Annie D. Tallent, *The Black Hills, the Last Hunting Ground of the Dakotahs* (St. Louis, 1899). As a reminiscence of Black Hills history written by the first white woman in the region, this book is excellent; as a history of the Little Bighorn, it slips into sloppy sentimentality, although Godfrey was the primary source. In relating how the news of the Custer disaster was received in the Black Hills, the writer, as one who was there, makes her slight contribution to Custer history.

�֍   �֍   ✖

THE 20TH CENTURY HISTORIANS

Unlike the participants in the Little Bighorn campaign and their friends, the writers of the 20th century have had no perceptible reason to become emotionally involved in the events of 1876. Yet partisanship in this century has been even more bitter than in the last. Loudest were the Custerphobes of the 1920's and 1930's, led by Frederick F. Van de Water, E. A. Brininstool, C. E. De-Land, and Fred Dustin.[20] Although they quarrelled incessantly among themselves over details and interpretations, they shared a passionate, almost unhealthy, hatred of Custer. They examined every shred of evidence through lenses tinted by this hatred, and their writings pronounce venomous judgment upon Custer for virtually every known fact of his life. How men could work up and sustain such intense emotion over a figure from the past poses an intriguing topic for speculation, one that Prof. Norman Maclean of the University of Chicago has been exploring for some years.

In contrast, Col. W. A. Graham approached the subject with an objectivity almost as passionate as the prejudice of the others. To Graham, objectivity meant not only a scrupulously open mind in the handling of evidence, but also the avoidance, in presentation, of all

[20]Van de Water: *Glory Hunter: A Life of General Custer* (Indianapolis and New York, 1934).

Brininstool: *A Trooper with Custer, and Other Historic Incidents of the Battle of the Little Big Horn* (Columbus, 1926; 2nd ed., Harrisburg, 1952); *Major Reno Vindicated* (Hollywood, 1935); "Unwritten Seventh Cavalry History, "*Middle Border Bulletin,* IV (1925); "Custer Battle Water Party: The Experience of Theodore W. Goldin . . ." *Hunter-Trader-Trapper,* August 1932; "DuRudio's Thrilling Escape . . ." *ibid.,* March 1933; "With Col. Varnum at the Little Big Horn . . ." *ibid.,* June & July 1927.

Deland: *The Sioux Wars,* South Dakota Historical Society, *Collections,* XV (1930); XVII (1934).

Dustin: *The Custer Fight* (Hollywood, 1936); *The Custer Tragedy* (Ann Arbor, 1939); *Echoes from the Little Big Horn Fight* (Saginaw, 1953).

judgments and most interpretations. He was concerned almost exclusively with events, not motivations. His books and articles,[21] for all their sterility of style, were nonetheless refreshing amid the bitter outpourings of his contemporaries, and also undeniably the greatest contributions of his era to unravelling the events of the Little Bighorn campaign. In his later years, however, Graham, perhaps partly as a result of long association with Brininstool and Dustin, gravitated perceptibly toward their views, but his writings failed to reflect the full measure of this trend in his thinking.[22]

The Custerphobes of the 1920's and 1930's, especially Van de Water, who unlike the rest was not a one-topic historian, expressed the dominant tone of biographical writing of the period. It was a time for tearing down heroes and exposing the clay feet of the idols venerated by past generations. But there were voices crying in the wilderness—Frederick Dellenbaugh and Frazier Hunt wrote laudatory biographies[23]—and Gen. Hugh S. "Iron Pants" Johnson, reviewing Van de Water's *Glory Hunter*, demonstrated in swashbuckling prose that the debunkers had by no means won the day. "As history," wrote Johnson, "this book is just adverse advocacy. As biography, it is merely muckraking. As military criticism, it

[21]*Story of the Little Big Horn* (New York, 1926; 2nd ed., Harrisburg, 1945); *The Custer Myth: A Source Book of Custeriana* (Harrisburg, 1953); *The Reno Court of Inquiry* (Harrisburg, 1954).

[22]This judgment is based on extensive correspondence between Graham and the author between 1949 and 1954.

[23]Frederick S. Dellenbaugh, *George Armstrong Custer* (New York, 1926); Frazier Hunt, *Custer, The Last of the Cavaliers* (New York, 1928).

sounds like the musings of a daisy-crunching doughboy." Van de Water had done "that which even an acorn-eating Digger Indian would scorn to consider—scalp an heroic warrior found dead on the field of honor."[24]

In a class by himself stood Dr. Charles Kuhlman, who brought a superior mind to the study of the Custer Fight. After deafness ended a promising academic career, he moved to Billings, Montana, where he earned a small income as a gardener and devoted the remainder of his life to seeking a satisfactory explanation of the mystery of the Little Bighorn. The results of his labor display the most profound and complex logic, and even for the deepest student require diligent study.[25] Although a defender of Custer, his chief purpose was to work out the events that occurred on the battle ridge. But even such carefully reasoned conclusions as he set forth failed to win widespread agreement. After briefly enjoying a reputation as the final authority, Kuhlman, too, came ultimately to represent simply one more point of view.

And so the capacity of George Armstrong Custer to surround himself with mystery and to inspire emotional extremes has persisted almost a century after his death. True, there have been signs of moderation and realism. Edgar I. Stewart published an authoritative and balanced history of the Little Bighorn in 1955, and Jay Monaghan in 1959 produced a biography that for the first time por-

[24]"Gen. Johnson Rides to the Defense," *Today Magazine,* Dec. 29, 1934.

[25]*Custer and the Gall Saga* (Billings, Mont., 1940); *Legend into History: The Custer Mystery* (Harrisburg, 1951); *Did Custer Disobey Orders at the Battle of the Little Big Horn?* (Harrisburg, 1957).

trayed Custer as a mortal with both faults and virtues.[26] But it is unlikely that such realists will ever do much to abate the Custer Controversy.

[26]Edgar I. Stewart, *Custer's Luck* (Norman, 1955); Jay Monaghan, *Custer: The Life of General George Armstrong Custer* (Boston, 1959).

INDEX

Custer and the Great Controversy

Index

Fourth Cavalry, 83
French, Capt. T. H., 59n9, 106
Frett, John, 59n9; testimony at Reno
  Court, 60
Frost, Dr. Lawrence A., ix
Fry, Gen. J. B., sketch, 65n18; defends
  Custer, 65-66; 67-69, 74

Galaxy, 52
Gall, 83, 85, 87; account of Little Big-
  horn, 107-10; 143, 155, 158
Garland, Hamlin, 11-12
Genin, Fr. J. B. M., 96-97
Gerard, F. F., 37, 59n9; testimony at
  Reno Court, 60; 150
Ghent, W. J., 78
Gibbon, Col. John, 21, 22, 24, 27, 31,
  32, 42, 59n9, 69, 75, 81-82; 138,
  142, 148, 149, 151
Gibson, Lt. F. M., 59n9
Gilbert, Lyman D., 58-61
Godfrey, Edward S., 27n5, 59n9; testi-
  mony at Reno Court, 60; 62; article
  in *Century*, 65; 67, 68, 74-77, 95n-
  12, 107, 109-10, 125-26, 130, 144n-
  32
Goes Ahead, 138-40
Graham, Col. W. A., ix, 62-63, 75, 78-
  79, 86, 106n21, 131n15, 137-38,
  144n32, 147, 163-64
Grant, U. S., 30; press attacks, 39-41;
  views on Little Bighorn, 44-45; 48
Grass, John, 110
Grinnell, G. B., 112-13, 131
Grouard, Frank, 161
Gurley, Lt. C. L., 77

Hairy Moccasin, 138-40
Half-Yellow-Face, 138-40
Hampton, Maj. Gen. Wade, 16
Hanson, J. M., 33n5, 36n10
Hare, Lt. L. R., 59n9, 150
Hayes, Pres. R. B., 57
Helena Herald, 32, 33-34

Helena Independent, 32
Herendeen, George, 59n9, 148, 150,
  151
Holley, Frances C., 149-50
Horned Horse, 91-92; account of Lit-
  tle Bighorn, 92-93
Hughes, Col. R. P., 43n12; defends
  Terry, 67-71; sketch, 67n19; 74-76
Humfreville, J. L., 161-62
Hump, 100
Hunt, Frazier, 164
Hutchins, J. S., ix
Hunter, William, 91
Hyde, G.E., 113-14

Ice Bear, 91
Indian testimony, 15, 78, 85-114;
  evaluation of, 85-90; 114
Indianapolis Sentinel, 39-40, 43,
  154n11
Inkpaduta, 91, 131
Inman, Col. Henry, 127n8, 157
Inside-the Mouth, 138
Iron Star, 84
Iron Thunder, 100

Jackson, William, 151
Johnson, Gen. Hugh S., 164-65
Johnson, Roy P., ix
Johnson, W. F., 160
Johnston, Gen. J. E., 46
*Journal of the Military Service Institu-
  tion of the United States*, 68

Kellogg, Mark, 30-31; 37, 148, 160
Kelsey, D. M., 157
Keogh, Capt. Myles, 82, 105, 108, 143,
  145
Kill Eagle, account of Little Bighorn,
  90
King, Col. J. H., 57
Korn, Gustave, 144-45
Kuhlman, Dr. Charles, ix, 70n23, 78,
  89, 103, 105-06, 165

Custer and the Great Controversy

Index